Rest Is Best

By Z. Rinpoche

First Edition 2025
Short Moments Media: Mill Valley, California USA 2025

ISBN 978-1-7371596-3-6

Rest Is Best

Contents

Editor's Introduction   *vii*

Section One: Introduction to the Wisdom Teachings   11

   1. Spontaneous and Obvious at All Times   12
   2. Exalted and Extraordinary   19
   3. Rest Is Best!   25
   4. Giving and Receiving   31
   5. One Simple Step at a Time   37
   6. The Under-Mutter   43
   7. The Moonlight Shining in Countless Ponds   49
   8. To Go to Any Lengths in Practice   55

Section Two: Educating and Sustaining Ourselves   61

   9. The Reality of Who We Are   62
   10. Wisdom-Exaltation and Sublime Activities   68
   11. Self-Compassion   74
   12. A Feast of Delight   80
   13. Our Genuine Self   86
   14. We Know That We Don't Know!   92
   15. Peaceful Mind   97
   16. The Wisdom of Discernment   103

Section Three: A Growing Familiarity   109

    17. The Road Less Traveled By   110
    18. Ultimate Comfort   116
    19. Vulnerability   122
    20. A Comprehensive Intelligence   128
    21. What Connects Everyone   134
    22. Inconceivable   140
    23. Self-Educating   146
    24. A Sense of Delight   152

Section Four: Showing Up Fully   159

    25. The Desire for Experience   160
    26. Generosity   165
    27. The Union of Opposites   170
    28.Showing Up   175
    29. Workability   181
    30. Unbidden and Non-Grasping Love   187
    31. A Life of Exciting Mystery   194
    32. The Ultimate Solution   200

Section Five: Going to Any Lengths   207

    33. Wisdom Agency   208
    34. What We Were Born to Be   214
    35. Omniscience   219
    36. The Primordial Sound   224
    37. The Breath Practice   231
    38. The Twelve Empowerments   237
    39. In My Essence I Am Free   245
    40. Great Love and Great Bliss   250
    41. This One Great Choice   256

Further Resources   261

Editor's Introduction

With great gratitude and enthusiasm, we in the Short Moments community are now offering this new book, *Rest Is Best*, from Z. Rinpoche to the reading public. The book consists of the key points taken from a number of talks that Z. Rinpoche gave in 2022, 2023 and 2024.

The usual word for a communication between a speaker and an audience is indeed "a talk," however, more specifically these sharings from Rinpoche are an evocation. In an evocation, the realization of the teacher is being evoked in the student. What is inherently present in the student is being brought to light—evoked—by a compassionate teacher.

We offer our heartfelt thanks to Rinpoche for these wonderful evocations which have been of such great service to so many. Rinpoche is a lineage-successor in the Dzogchen and Mahamudra lineages, and in that capacity has been enjoined by her guru, Wangdor Rimpoche, to bring the Dzogchen and Mahamudra teachings to a wider world. Dzogchen, the "Great Completion" or the "Great Perfection," and Mahamudra, "The Great Seal," in Tibetan, have been associated with the Tibetan Buddhist tradition for many centuries, but the teachings are now being introduced to a much more extensive audience.

The evocations that were selected for inclusion in this book are extremely powerful, and also very specific to the moment. Rinpoche goes into all of the evocations she gives with no plan or agenda, and responds skillfully to what is directly needed by the participants in that time, place and circumstance. The teachings are in plain and simple English, but that does not mean that a newcomer to the teachings, or even an old-timer, will find everything to be completely understandable from the outset.

Some mulling over, contemplation and rereading may be required in order that the profundity of the teachings can become obvious.

The warm, loving and informal style of the oral teachings is retained in this written rendition, and the language has not been formalized. As the emphasis here is on the key points of the teachings, each paragraph is very direct and concise. In fact, each individual paragraph could be read as a teaching in itself.

There will be a number of terms which will require some defining and explaining. First there is the word "Dzogchen," which is the core teaching that is being referenced. There are also the essential elements of that teaching including "open intelligence," "awareness," "data," "points of view," "reification," "rest," "resting," "bodhicitta," "tonglen," "the heart essence," and others.

Then there are words that are being used in an unconventional way, such as "mind," "reason" and "binary thinking," and also descriptives such as "causal," "rationalistic" and "oppositional" that may require some clarification. All of these terms are defined in the text itself and should become clearer with increased familiarity through rereading.

One key aspect, maybe the key aspect, is the repetition the reader will encounter in the book. The same teachings will be repeated in different contexts from a slightly different angle. This is in no way an accident. The key points are presented again and again and gradually become more familiar, until they become trusted pointers and guides. Repetition furthers, and for a reader who is open to repetition, there are many riches to be gathered.

And yes, openness. That may be the most important capacity to bring to the reading of this book: simply being open and available to ideas that may not be immediately familiar. There are some unaccustomed teachings here that a reader might not have encountered before. But please know that openness is the welcome friend that readily opens hearts and minds and clarifies what had previously been unclear.

Once again, we are so grateful to Z. Rinpoche for this wonderful offering to the world, and it is our hope that you will benefit as much from the reading (and rereading!) of the book as we on the editorial team have from the preparing of it.

Section One

INTRODUCTION TO THE WISDOM TEACHINGS

1. Spontaneous and Obvious at All Times   12

2. Exalted and Extraordinary   19

3. Rest Is Best!   25

4. Giving and Receiving   31

5. One Simple Step at a Time   37

6. The Under-Mutter   43

7. The Moonlight Shining in Countless Ponds   49

8. To Go to Any Lengths in Practice   55

SPONTANEOUS AND OBVIOUS AT ALL TIMES

CHAPTER ONE

The impact of these teachings is so ongoingly profound for me; I never tire of their brilliance and I never tire of the resonance of their impact within me. I can't imagine what I would be doing in life if I hadn't had the honor and privilege of being exposed to these teachings.

When we first come to a wisdom teaching, we are being pointed towards understanding who we are. As we practice, our mind gradually opens up, and we begin to see that, in its essence, all that we are perceiving is vast and deep. The openness of the vast blue sky is one of the key metaphors that illustrates this view. Over time, as practice deepens, this vastness becomes more evident, and we become more and more familiar with what the vastness and depth reveal.

When we are introduced to open intelligence, we are being introduced to our own nature as open intelligence, even though at first we may only be able to connect with it briefly. Nevertheless, we have seen that our true identity is available to us and that we are being invited to recognize it more profoundly.

All there is, is stainless, flawless ever-present open intelligence. If we choose to relax body and mind completely and rest naturally as open intelligence for short moments repeated many times, open intelligence will become more and more evident. When we rest as ourselves, we don't have to be anything in particular.

When the terms "rest" or "resting" are used, they mean to leave everything just *as it is*. We keep it simple: resting, or we could also say relaxing, for short moments, many times, and not being distracted or taken over by what is arising in the mind. Short moments of rest increasingly open up the balanced view, clarity and insight of open intelligence. Short moments of rest repeated again and again become spontaneous, and clarity becomes increasingly obvious until it is evident at all times. This is the short moments practice.

⊜⊐⊜

With continued practice, we realize that when we rest, we are resting as what is, *as it is*. We don't ever have to struggle to try to force ourselves into a state; we simply rest as what is. The recognition of what is isn't merely a passing experience; it is a realization that is always-on, and one that is totally authentic and natural.

So, simply relax and remain in your own open-intelligence-place just *as it is*. When we rest as we are, we realize that we have tremendous energy, and when we rest as that energy, we come to realize that this energy is our true mind. Then we understand that our body and mind are actually a flow of energy. Well, it isn't really an "energy" as that word is commonly understood. It is simply what is.

When we are open, and we show up as we truly are, we realize that the mind is vast and deep. The mind doesn't reside in the brain, and we have a lot more going for us than just the brain! The brain is a brilliant processor of information; however, this enormous capacity of the brain is actually minimal when compared to the tremendous energy of an intelligence that is beyond comprehension.

Ordinary intelligence could be viewed in terms of high IQ or low IQ or anywhere in between, but open intelligence is so vast and so deep that it is beyond explanation, comprehension or measurement. This incomprehensible intelligence guarantees us a life that can serve us completely as well as serve those around us.

Fortunately, resting as open intelligence—also called "awareness"—for short moments many times is perfect as a practice for anyone in the world. Does it mean that a person who is resting is jumping around full of joy all the time? No, it doesn't mean that. What it means is that there is a depth of realization in which we take account of ourselves in a very direct and fundamental way.

How many people are there who sit down and actually take account of themselves and of their entire life? It is probably quite rare, but when we use the practice to inquire and to see specifically what our life has consisted of, we are taking account of ourselves in an honest and straightforward way. This is a radical act. So, we can congratulate ourselves, because we have started the process of actually inquiring into the most profound qualities of a human life.

Not only that, we're doing it in a very systematic way. Through the teachings and the practice we have the tools needed for this inquiry. In taking account of ourselves, we are gracing ourselves with a great gift. The more that we inquire into our true being, the more we come to know about life in a simple, direct and joyous way.

To realize something as magnificent as this—but something that may seem so distant that it seems totally impossible—requires one simple step at a time. No matter how huge this or any other endeavor seems to be, and no matter how overwhelming it is, it will only be realized one simple step at a time, one short moment at a time.

The teachings that lead to this realization may seem unclear and somewhat hard to understand, but they are in fact very simple— not always easy, but simple. For myself, I needed something simple. I needed simple truths that I know can operate in my life.

At first, it may sometimes seem like nothing is happening in the practice of resting naturally, but everything is taking place that needs to take place. We continue to rest naturally for short moments many times until the rest is spontaneous and obvious at all times. When this actually takes place, more wisdom and skillful means become available to us, skillful means that can very often be of specific service to others. Indeed, rest is best.

The energy that from the very beginning of our lives has been called by many names is in fact a single energy, the energy of our aliveness—also called awareness or open intelligence. That energy is all-good, all-embracing, all-loving. The recognition of that energy provides an invitation to exaltation, regardless of what is occurring. We no longer have to dwell on painful things that have happened in our lives or hope for better things. We do not want to dwell in the realm of hope and fear.

The teachings work, and I know this for sure through my own experience. At one time I saw things as being determined by cause and effect and divided into aspects of good and bad, happy and sad, pleasurable and not pleasurable. For quite a while this was very troublesome for me, but the teachings changed all that for me.

When we first come to the practice, we may feel that there's something wrong with us, because we have all kinds of thoughts and emotions—data—that have been labeled all kinds of things. But when we rest and we see that everything is a point of light, including us as a point of light in a vast cosmos, then we can begin to see that we're not separate from the vast cosmos.

We can come alive to the reality that everything exhibits fundamental connection—the ocean, the trees, nature as a whole. Oh, their beauty . . . I revel in this magnificence with such awe, wonder and pleasure. It is such a gift to be in accord with nature, because after all, we are nature, and we, like nature, are intelligent. All of creation is the place of intelligence. How could we as human beings be left out?

In our teachings the word "data" refers to all thoughts, emotions, experiences, sensations, events and perceptions. Another phrase might be "points of view," but whatever term it may be, it refers to all perceived phenomena. We can stop for a minute and imagine all the data that exist, all the points in the universe, and in the same way see the entire universe as points of light.

The "points of light" would then be synonymous with "points of view" or "data" in this example. Of course, this isn't a comprehensive description of the truth; it's only an example to demonstrate what is being spoken about: that all of what appears is points of light not bounded by definitions or opinion. The key element of this is that data are inseparable from open intelligence. Data are the dynamic display of open intelligence.

With practice, there is less of a need to conform to conventional social norms. An example of conforming in my own life would have been for me to have entered into a lifestyle based on the expectations of my particular demographic and then to have tailored myself to those expectations. But I just couldn't do that, because I felt it would be inauthentic.

Even the thought of conforming to the norm made me feel extremely uncomfortable. I could not do it, because conforming would feel like a betrayal of my genuine nature. One can be one's authentic self without the need to edit oneself to fit established standards.

The impact of these teachings is so ongoingly profound for me; I never tire of their brilliance and I never tire of the resonance of their impact within me. I can't imagine what I would be doing in life if I hadn't had the honor and privilege of being exposed to these teachings. They state the same thing over and over again in multiple brilliant ways. Over and over again ongoingly, and then once again!

Repetition is key. Repetition is key. Repetition is key.

❖

We have been slowly trained up in becoming an individual being who is separate from other beings. With practice, however, there is no longer the same sense of being an individual. The assertion that "there is no longer the same sense of being an individual" can be a bit startling to hear! If it is startling, well, so what, that is just another point of view to rest with!

Generally, when we buy into all manner of things in which the culture has educated us, we often make ourselves into someone who is not genuine and authentic. This brings us suffering, because the truly authentic in us is not being heeded. We need to be ourselves in a genuine and authentic way and to not allow ourselves to be made into something that thoughts, emotions and reified thinking would lead us to believe we are. We have something so satisfying, fulfilling and rewarding within us, and in every single moment we are receiving this gift.

We have learned throughout our lives to reify thoughts, emotions, sensations and experiences. "To reify" means that we give people, places, things, thoughts, emotions and experiences—all data—an independent nature and then describe them from a vantage of separation. We give the thoughts and emotions a presence and power that they do not inherently have. Our way of being is then determined by thinking which only divides and describes. Prior to knowing any other way to be, the reification of thoughts, emotions, sensations and experiences has informed everything we do, but now through the practice we are making a different choice.

Through our practice we gradually free ourselves from the chaos brought about by reified thinking. We don't need to struggle to get into a state or try to control our body and mind. We don't need to try to see things in a new way; we simply rest as we are and as we have always been. There's no norm for anything. How could there be a norm when everything is indefinable and inexpressible?

EXALTED AND EXTRAORDINARY
CHAPTER TWO

We shine with an expressive heart. We're no longer giving ourselves a whipping every day because of what we think is wrong with us! Instead, we're resting. We are exalting ourselves.

In my earlier life, I didn't really have a framework for living, other than the conventional things like education, religion, career, family and so on. I didn't have a way of truly understanding my life, and because of that, I didn't really have a clear inner life, even though I had been a practitioner almost all of my life.

I *knew* I needed to connect with others who were understanding life in the same way I was, and I *knew* those people existed, and I *knew* I was going to find them. Thankfully, I eventually came to these teachings that made an incredible philosophy of life totally clear for me.

Through this wonderful short moments practice, an energy is recognized which comes alive in us. The practice builds gradually, even if sometimes the energy is not recognized. The presence of this energy is nevertheless undeniable, because it is the dynamic energy of who we are. Every single moment has this energy, so it is not like we have to go out and try to find it elsewhere.

What is being described here may sound at first very foreign, but the inherent understanding within ourselves is already present, albeit hidden by a lifetime of miseducation! Because we have this inherent understanding, the teachings can ring true when we first hear them. "Inherently having the understanding" is a good place to start!

It's important that in our practice we are facing everything about life, and that we are facing everything as it actually is, rather than as some make-believe world. The preciousness of who we are is slowly revealed. It isn't something we have not experienced already; we've only overlooked it or forgotten it.

In the course of practice, both positive and negative things will come up, and very often the negative things will not be very pleasant. So, not only do the negative things come up, but they can be very unpleasant and can affect life quite dramatically. In whatever way it may be, amidst the arising of the positive and the negative, we rest as we are for short moments, many times.

Through resting, a great deal is revealed, and everything comes about in great beauty and majesty. As we move along, we are shown gifts that are absolutely amazing, and we realize that all of these gifts are already within us. Our mind becomes beneficial in its orientation, but not through *trying* to be beneficial. The benefit comes about spontaneously, without effort and without trying to be one thing or another. In no longer choosing to revolve in a world of opposites, a broader and more comprehensive choice opens up.

⊜∞⊜

In engaging in this practice, we are completely changing the way we look at emotions. We go from looking at the emotions as something that is scary or overwhelming to realizing that we have a power much greater than these daunting emotions. We have often been frightened of some of our emotional energy, and we might have tried to deny it or avoid it.

But instead of engaging in denial or acceptance, how do we re-enliven our true nature? Simple. When agitating energy or any kind of energy comes up, we rest in the energy itself. We do not try to get away from it or get rid of it. We rest for short moments many times in the energy, as the energy.

The energy is the heart. The "heart" is not just a place in our body. It is the living force in us. We shine with a resplendent heart.

We're no longer giving ourselves a whipping every day because of what we think is wrong with us. Instead, we're resting as the resplendent heart. We are exalting ourselves.

When we have an emotion like anger coming up, we might think, "Oh, that's bad, I can't have any anger; I need to remain calm." There is the focus on positive and negative—the two poles of thinking about any thought or emotion. But with continued practice these reference points are no longer our focus. An emotion might come up, but it is no longer described in the way it was before, and it doesn't any longer have the power to control us or provoke us into disharmonious activity. With whatever comes up, its natural self-release is increasingly guaranteed.

We can only experience, examine and investigate one datum— one point of view—at a time. We only have one thought at a time, and there is the energetic impulse associated with it. Whatever it is, it is inseparable from this natural energy in us. If we rest, we're resting as the *energy* of the point of view rather than as the definition of the point of view. Whatever it is that we are thinking, assuming or naming, all data are equal to the vast expanse of our very own intelligence just *as it is*.

No matter how much in the past we have been taken over by data, when we begin to practice we begin to see more clearly the "under-mutter." There's the "mutter"—the points of view we can recognize—and then there's the under-mutter, the things that are hidden from us, the thoughts and emotions that are percolating far beneath the surface. It's these things that are hidden from us that we also need to come to terms with in order to be at peace.

Equal and even energy is the nature of our environment, including the environment of "ourselves." Equal and even energy. When we are thinking that something other than "equal and even" is going on, we are then interpreting the energy in a way that isn't accurate.

For example, something like anxiety can be looked at more and more from this new perspective. We can come to see something that we considered negative to be a form of natural energy, and not merely as something to be gotten rid of. Gaining this perspective is what the practice is about. There are these two perspectives: the reified one that we've been taught, and the one based on resting that is native to us and that reveals reality.

When we practice, we're actually practicing our genuine self-energy, which is the energy we ourselves truly are. We're not doing something that is esoteric and out of the ordinary. We are being the most "ordinary" we could ever be. What we truly are has been covered up and hidden from us. When we "ordinary" beings have come fully to terms with ourselves, we come to see how very exalted and extraordinary we are in that ordinariness.

If coming to this new perspective is important enough for us, we will practice no matter what, and we will grow in our practice even through pitfalls and dry spells. We flourish, even though we have made decisions in the past that sometimes didn't go so well for us. But no matter how it is or was, eventually we understand that everything in what we call "past" and "future" is this energy that is only present *right here.*

Each of us practices in our own unique way, and yet, we're all called to the same task, which is to examine the long-held idea that we are a solid thing. Through practice we gradually come to know that "being a solid thing" is not the case for us. The realization comes through baby steps, each tiny step along the way, each short moment. Each step in the short moments practice is founded in reality and provides something that can't be lost.

❀

It's not like we're going to have a final moment when all the thoughts and emotions are pacified and fixed for the better, because the appearances, whatever they are, may carry on in exactly the same way. Sometimes people think, "There's something wrong. Nothing has changed. I'm having all the same thoughts and emotions as before." However, all along, the nature of reality has remained equal and even in all the phenomena—in the beginning, middle and end. Every experience is always a call to gather more treasure that we already possess. We are being invited to no longer be distracted away from this realization.

Practice fully and joyfully, even when you don't feel like practicing. All is well. Your treasure chest is open for more inexhaustible treasure! The capacity of this chest grows and grows, so there's no way to exhaust the richness of who you are.

Everyone wants a little, or a lot, of love. We all need that so much, and we want it for ourselves and for others. Please be open to the possibility that the time will come when you're thinking about yourself in a compassionate and loving way that more and more includes not only yourself, but everyone, no matter whether they appear to be bitter enemies or best friends.

We might come to realize that we have been talking to ourselves and others very negatively—a situation that is unfortunately very, very common. It is natural that we would feel regretful about the way that we have sometimes treated ourselves and others, but now with practice we can be with ourselves and our feelings in a very beneficial way. We no longer have the need to control ourselves, because we can see that control is a much less effective response when compared to rest. More and more we become spontaneous and we give up trying to control our experience.

Just think about how much of life has been about making a concrete plan in order to obtain specific results. In rest, we have no concrete plan, and we come to see that we don't need one, because we are opening to the experience of "no goal, no place to travel to, no more learning," which means that there is nothing we need to acquire and that we are already whole and complete. We can continue to read and listen to the teachings, doing whatever we do to further our practice, but it's not about getting a diploma or reaching some sort of conclusive goal.

We do not need to be afraid of being spontaneous, and we can let things happen as they will. To be clear, letting things happen as they will does allow for planning as well in our practical day-to-day existence. If we require a great deal of organization in our daily life, with practice we're able to develop that beyond anything we previously thought possible. So, spontaneity does not exclude skilled preparation, planning and organization.

We are as we are. Some of us are naturally cheerful and enthusiastic, and others of us aren't. Whether enthusiastic or not, we all have moments in our lives where anything and everything can occur. But everything that occurs is appearing as the awareness that includes all phenomena. Always, in whatever is occurring, we have a home and a place of rest.

REST IS BEST!

CHAPTER THREE

It's not the kind of thing where you say, "I'm going to fulfill all my wishes and get everything I want." That isn't the case. Outwardly things may carry on as before, but now instead of thoughts and emotions causing so much pain and suffering, you will shine.

How do we get from being afflicted with raging emotions to being content in life? Then also, how do we get to the point of having no regrets, or, if there are regrets, to being able to fully be with them in a way that they become sparkling wisdom, which they have always been?

First of all, we don't want to engage in despair and defeat by not practicing. Wisdom is what we really need, and not some cooked-up fantasy based on what we have taken our thoughts and emotions to be. We need to resolve confusion through practice. Anger, irritation and annoyance have to be cut at the root so that they can manifest their wisdom. Instead of trying to avoid these emotions or eliminating them from one's life, they are understood for what they are.

Annoyance, irritation, loathing—the emotion can be called all kinds of things—but it so often boils down essentially to anger. When we get annoyed or irritated, there is some vestige of anger coming up. The point of observing and coming to know all afflictive emotions, also called the poisons, is to discover their inherent wisdom. We need to re-understand the energy and to cut the poisons at the root. When they appear, we rest.

If irritation or annoyance come up—that little spark where our eyes narrow and there's the feeling that we've described as anger—do we try to get rid of what we're feeling? No, we rest in the energy itself. We rest in the energy as the energy.

We have been trained to believe that anger is something that it actually is not. We have learned that it is an energy that can destroy us, but to believe this is a very tough way to live. What do we have as a solution? Rest is best. That's what our solution is: rest is best. We rest, because wisdom is found in the rest.

❧❦❧

With that first spark of anger, we have the opportunity to make a choice: are we going to practice, or not? If we choose to indulge in the anger through misunderstanding the energy, then our mind will cloud with anger, and we will be continuing to train ourselves further in what has been so painful for us. To see anger for what it is, and through that to cut it at the root, is a very powerful act. When we cut off irritation and anger at the root, we really start to see the suffering that anger, revenge and hostility have brought us.

As we proceed in practice, we can begin to laugh at ourselves about the times in the past when we thought we would never be able to be free of the irritation. What a relief to no longer be burdened with that. Instead of irritation and frustration, more and more we feel enthusiasm. To have enthusiasm for life is so very precious. We become acquainted with the tremendous energy in us, and as we do so, we begin to have a lot of vitality. This vitality wakes us up and allows us to be deeply in touch with what we are feeling.

When we talk about wisdom-exaltation, sublime activities and great bliss, these are all to be found within. It's not some kind of split-off state and not a matter of getting away from anything. Our understanding, recognition and realization of what actually is are being evoked. This is a great gift.

It's not the kind of thing where you say, "I'm going to fulfill all my wishes and get everything I want." That isn't the case. Outwardly things may carry on as before, but now instead of thoughts and emotions causing so much pain and suffering, you will shine.

At this point in my life, I can definitely say that I am one hundred percent happy and grateful for having committed my life to the practice. I know I made the right choice, no matter what I heard from other folks. And so, in that same way, we stand up for ourselves and we remain who we are, no matter what the criticism or misunderstanding we may face.

I knew very little about Tibetan Buddhism or Tibetans when I met my gurus, Minling Trichen Rinpoche and Wangdor Rimpoche, but I could feel incredible love in them. My own gurus and the other wonderful grandfather gurus from Tibet supported me in my practice, and they have so very much influenced my life. They are all so extraordinary in their capacity for loving. If we want to know what realization is in a simple way, we could say that it is love—simply that: love. Wangdor Rimpoche in particular was a very peaceful emanation of the teachings, and at the same time he showed himself to me fully in all of his many human aspects.

I reflect often on the beings who cared about us so much that they ensured that we would have the teachings. They followed their inner knowing, their insight and their clarity, which are all the very nature of realization itself. They followed them unerringly, instead of using assumptions and conventions to define everything.

When the Chinese invaded Tibet, my guru, Wangdor Rimpoche, and many others felt compelled to leave Tibet. Due to the dire nature of the circumstances, Wangdor Rimpoche ended up carrying his guru, Thuksey Rinpoche, on his back all the way to India. This long and very difficult journey consisted of many short moments. That's what it was: a whole journey filled with rest for short moments many times, despite the enormous challenges.

We don't need to try to be something we are not, like, say, trying to become a Tibetan. We aren't Tibetans. The teachings are to be taught according to the culture in which people who are receiving those teachings are living. We each have different propensities and different patterns. According to our propensities, we choose different teachings. Everyone is meeting teachings every day anyway, whether they are teachings of the conventional, reified culture or they are Dzogchen teachings.

Here we're practicing Dzogchen, but in other places people are practicing other things. We have these teachings that are being spoken about here, but there are other teachings for the people who want to practice something else. Whatever path we choose, the more we practice the more we're able to go to any teaching and cultivate what is good for us.

Just as there were specifically Tibetan capacities within the unique culture of Tibet, we also have our own capacities that are equally powerful to face the challenges we have. There are possibilities for the teachings around the globe in this era which may not even look like the teachings in Tibet. We don't know exactly how things in the world will unfold, but no matter how or what, we continue to show up in the way that is most skillful.

❀

What you are reading in this book is a Dzogchen teaching. Dzogchen means "Great Completion" or "Great Perfection" because it sees beings as perfect, and it always upholds the perfection of beings. "Great Completion" means the utter completion of intelligence. Dzogchen not only shows us that we are innately complete, but it has an exact method that delivers that result.

Dzogchen has many tools, with the primary tool being the practice of short moments many times. That practice helps us train our minds so that we don't any longer put so much energy into thoughts and emotions. Through that practice we know for sure what's good for us. That's the way we live our lives, and that's the way we practice. We are less self-protective, less emotionally reactive and we go from happiness to happiness, instead of from one desire for experience to another desire for experience.

For many centuries Dzogchen has been associated with Tibetan Buddhism, and sometimes Dzogchen is still taught within that context. However, in these teachings here, Dzogchen is taught independently of Tibetan Buddhism. We are part of the Dzogchen community, but these teachings are a unique expression, you could say, one that is understandable to a modern audience.

There are so many Dzogchen practices, but my teachers asked me to focus on a specific type of practice for a specific type of practitioner. I didn't know how it would unfold when we started giving the teachings in this way, but I just showed up and went forward. This is a very simplified approach to Dzogchen, and this simplified approach is something that was encouraged in me when I met my guru, Wangdor Rimpoche. This approach could also be called "education in the nature of mind."

Dzogchen is unique in its simplicity of practice and its potency. The depth of what is realized is completely beyond any kind of intelligence that is normally attributed to human beings. We can look at the intelligence that is brought about through Dzogchen as something that goes far beyond reified thinking.

There are very few people who are ever introduced to Dzogchen and very few who even come into contact with it or hear the word "Dzogchen." Dzogchen also wasn't practiced by so many people in its Tibetan setting, but from those few who did practice, many became enlightened. The fact that even one became enlightened gives us hope, because if there was even one, then we have the opportunity as well! In certain circumstances there might not be any examples of enlightenment around us, and yet we still have the opportunity.

I find this Dzogchen teaching to be of such significance that I really don't have the words for it. It is so very, very important. There are amazing things happening today around the globe and there are incredible people who are contributing in incredible ways. These moments of authentic engagement are of urgent necessity. Something precious is being gifted to the world.

GIVING AND RECEIVING

CHAPTER FOUR

The giving and receiving leads to finding no separation between beings. We share what will alleviate suffering and bring happiness—true happiness, always-on happiness that warms us on the inside and warms everything we see.

It is important for us as practitioners to have an introduction to the brilliant practice of giving and receiving, called "tonglen" in Tibetan. We could begin with a quotation from His Holiness the Fourteenth Dalai Lama, who said,

"Tonglen has a wealth of meaning that is difficult to convey succinctly, though the ideas it conveys are universally understood. It connotes love, affection, kindness, gentleness, generosity of spirit and warmheartedness. It is also used as a term of both sympathy and endearment. It does not imply pity. On the contrary, tonglen denotes a feeling of connection with others, reflecting its origin in empathy."

The Dalai Lama's way of practicing tonglen is to take in the suffering of the entire world and then give out his endless immense compassion; however, for a new practitioner it is of course fitting to begin the practice on a much smaller scale. The practice is based on taking in the suffering of another, and then giving out one's love, affection and kindness to the individual or suffering circumstance we are meditating on. Tonglen is a practice of giving and receiving, giving and receiving, giving and receiving. It is both the source and result of patience, tolerance, forgiveness and all good qualities and all good things.

I would suggest a simple approach to the practice at first. For instance, when I began practicing tonglen, I had the flu and was very sick. I thought, "Lots of people in the world have the flu right now, and they're suffering, just like I am. I'm going to take

31

in their pain and suffering while giving as much love, connection and empathy as I can." As much *empathy*, not just sympathy. Those two are quite different. I once read that empathy is like jumping in the hole with the other person, totally being with them where they are and relating to them from their perspective.

Taking in and giving out, we feel a sense of preciousness and calm that we may not have known before. Tonglen is an approach that requires gentleness with ourselves and a sense of knowing who we are and wanting to know more about others. It's about our deepest form of relationship with ourselves and others. Tonglen is a very simple practice, yet it is extremely powerful. It's important to get started with it.

❦

When we give, we give what we can identify in ourselves as good—happiness, pleasure, joy of life, gratitude for the practice and everything that brings benefit. We take in the pain of others' experience, and we give out what would comfort and soothe and bring well-being to them. As we continue with the practice, the result in our everyday life is that in any situation we will know what to do and how to act. We find a way of being that is so very much needed in this time in which we live.

Tonglen is not a matter of pity, but of compassion. Compassion cannot be generated only through thinking about it or *trying* to generate it. It is not a matter of trying, but of practicing. The practice of tonglen creates warmheartedness in us that is obvious. With love, affection, kindness, gentleness and generosity of spirit, indeed, we become very warmhearted.

We breathe in the pain and negativity or whatever else is causing suffering for another, and we breathe out empathy and compassion. We allow the breath to ride in and out—riding the breath in and out, in and out, giving and receiving, giving and receiving. Through breathing in and breathing out and in taking in the suffering and giving out the ultimate compassion, we give to ourselves as well as to another. It changes our relationship with others.

Initially we may need to engage in a formal practice, but the more spontaneous we become, the less we have the need to do so. What had been cultivated in tonglen becomes spontaneous and free, because now we don't have to *practice* anything. This is what is called non-meditation, which means that we have no need to set aside a period for practice and meditation, because we're continuously in that stance of giving and receiving. We become thereby more and more spontaneous in our approach to life, and whatever is present right now for us is what we are responding to.

This is a way of life, and it can take hold in us to the degree that meditation is spontaneously present. I believe this is more possible today than it ever has been. Why is that? Because we need it so desperately now in our suffering world.

Tonglen is something that can be practiced anywhere, and in practicing tonglen wherever we are, we grow in strength. When we begin tonglen, it involves actively using our imagination to bring specific situations to mind, but the need to purposely imagine a scenario eventually lessens as the giving and receiving become more spontaneous.

When we actively bring situations and people to mind, we bring in not only the painful experience of another, but also of ourselves, because we are part of the same suffering. We as humans are united in our experience of suffering. The giving and receiving practice leads to finding no separation between beings. We share what will alleviate suffering and bring happiness, true happiness, always-on happiness that warms us on the inside and warms everything we see.

Inseparable from the self-perfected qualities and activities of beneficial potency is the passionate desire to benefit all. The best word for that is *bodhicitta*—the deep desire in one's life to spontaneously benefit all. It means not only being compassionate, but also having the wish to free all beings from suffering and to bring them to enlightenment. The ultimate bodhicitta is always-on tonglen.

We are called to practice tonglen, and to the degree that we practice, to that degree we realize the results. We can imagine our own pain and the pain of others, and that is the beginning of tonglen: imagining our own pain and imagining the pain of others, and then bringing in the pain and giving out good wishes, love and healing.

With the world in the state that it is in, having some way to soothe our experience and that of others is so crucial. This practice is going to become more and more important to practitioners. There are plenty of opportunities to practice tonglen, and we can also practice with those we don't like at all! Maybe it's the head of a country or someone else, but whoever it might be, we take in all the pain and suffering, and give out all goodness.

Many people are coming together around the globe to relieve suffering, and practicing tonglen is itself such a powerful way to relieve suffering. When I see young people today, this first generation of digital natives, I can see the uniqueness of their being, their exceptional way of seeing the world, their connection with others around the world, and their increasing capacity to be at ease with seemingly radical statements like some of the ones that are being made here.

I feel very confident that these teachings can serve many people, especially in these times when we so much need to connect with each other. I am trusting that someday all human beings will be born knowing who they are, and that they will be able to sincerely practice tonglen and provide ultimate bodhicitta. This is what I would so love to see in the world.

Tonglen is unbearable compassion for our-self, our *Self*—Self with a capital S. When the phrase "unbearable compassion" is used, people generally don't like the word "unbearable." When I first heard "unbearable compassion," I thought, "How would I get anything done if it is unbearable?" I'm very literal in my thinking, and I want the exact definition of words. One definition that became clear for me is that unbearability is the ever-present expression of perfect love in the world. I came to see that there's never a moment when unbearable compassion isn't present.

I knew that I really wanted to practice for all beings, but I also felt, "Well, do I really want to start in such a big way?" I needed to start with something practical rather than just go all out. From there I wanted to move to the point where I could take in everything and relate to the state of the world and all her beings. So, I did that; I practiced sequentially until I did reach the point of practicing this way, and now I'm never not practicing tonglen.

For me, that's the way it works: do the practice and the results come along, and after a while, one is not looking for results or even noticing them. Everything just is *as it is*. Everything is doable and workable. We already have the wisdom; we'll know what we need to know when we need to know it. Each of us needs to progress at her or his own pace in this.

To practice tonglen requires awareness of the suffering of others, but it may begin with becoming aware of their suffering through our own suffering. Tonglen is such a rich practice, because it raises our awareness about the suffering that is so very present for so many in the world. We can give ourselves compassion through sharing it with others. We can offer our compassion to others, and as we perfect the practice, more and more bodhicitta and wisdom-exaltation are revealed to us. This is the quality of realization: bodhicitta and wisdom-exaltation.

Usually we don't hear much in life about exaltation or being exalted; however, we are exalted beings, and as we practice, we come to know ourselves as exalted. As exalted beings, there comes a point where bodhicitta is very present for us. When we walk, we are walking as bodhicitta, and as we breathe, we are breathing as bodhicitta. In taking our last breath before death, that last breath is breathed as bodhicitta.

ONE SIMPLE STEP AT A TIME

CHAPTER FIVE

It becomes possible to rest distinctly in everything—which means everything that we've thought is awful and everything that we've thought is wonderful, because it isn't about thinking! The ultimate level of truth is not about thinking and is far beyond any kind of mental fabrication.

We are happiest when we are our genuine self, and the teachings of Dzogchen are about being one's genuine self. Some might feel a bit uncomfortable with some of the aspects of the teachings, because the focus is not only on who we are, but also on who we are not, and that can bring up some resistance in people. However, seeing who we are not is just as important as seeing who we are.

The ultimate level of truth is always showing itself to us. The more we can rest and love ourselves, the more we realize that the ultimate level of truth is not different from who we are. We're learning here about who we are, just as in growing up in a binary-related culture we have learned to be who we are *not*.

In a binary-related culture we're told that there are certain things that are negative and which don't belong. This assumption can be very disconcerting and can lead to a lot of confusion. However, when this assumption is intensely inquired into, we come to see that there are not in essence two different aspects of positive and negative.

As the terms "binary," "causal" "and "rationalistic" will be used frequently in the book, it is important to define them. These terms each refer to the vantage of seeing things dualistically and in terms of opposites—rather than as a whole. When we look through a binary lens, we divide things into good and bad, wished for and not wished for, black and white, pleasure and pain, subject and object and all the other pairs of opposites.

In a rationalistic/binary view, everything exists in the context of space and time, cause and effect, past and future, rather than as the nondual open intelligence that it is. Everything is seen through a causal lens and as a binary construct that includes reward and punishment, comparison and competition, realization and no realization. Oppositional, causal and rationalistic thinking is then applied to each experience. All of these describe a false view and a false self.

We need to learn to rest with the things we don't want, instead of feeling averse to them, and to rest with wanting to get more of what we think is good. In Dzogchen, things are no longer seen in a causal or binary way. It doesn't matter what its name is, whether positive or negative, everything is pristine open intelligence.

Anything that appears is the magic of ultimate wisdom itself, and when we bloom into the radiance of our sparkling wisdom, it becomes possible to live in a way that is not describable. When people know what to do and how to act in the moment, it may become obvious to some others that this is so. When this capacity is recognized in a particular person, it is possible that these others will be inspired by it.

❧∞❧

In a reified, binary, rationalistic view, we perceive what is present as something that has a phenomenal cause and effect, and that whatever the phenomenon is, it has an opposite. For example, whatever confusion is, it has its opposite, and whatever realization is, it has its opposite. In Dzogchen we develop the mind of unity and the supreme view by simply resting in the energy that is present in both. We can rest as the energy that is present and really never need to talk about something being "opposite."

We're so often engaged in opposing something in ourselves, and it becomes tiring. Things come up for us that we think we have to push back against so that we won't have them anymore, but in resting, we know that this fight is no longer necessary. We are already pure and perfect as we are, and we don't need to get rid of anything.

Pure and perfect open intelligence is only right now; it's never in the future or the past, because it has no future or past. Everything we have thought about ourselves in the past was due to a hardcore training in binary thinking, but when we rest, we realize that we are not something born from causes and circumstances. There may be things that are affecting us, but the solution is not to be found in trying to get rid of those things.

So, when we have something come up such as disdain or contempt, we rest in the energy and as the energy, and not in the image itself. Again, we rest in the energy and not in the definition. This insight is a means to modify our perspective, and modify our perspective permanently.

It becomes possible to rest distinctly in everything, which means everything that we've thought is awful and everything that we've thought is wonderful, *because it isn't about thinking*! The ultimate level of truth is not about thinking and is far beyond any kind of mental fabrication.

When people are devoted to serving others, that kindness is coming from a space of being clear and open. The clearer and more open we are, the more we can see everything *as it is*. We can see that there is nothing that is not equal and even. We see everything, including things that had been deemed negative, as pure and open. That becomes the central truth of our lives. "Unborn, pure, equal and even" is then how we perceive the nature of things.

We view ourselves and the world from the vantage of bodhicitta. We burn inside with a unique kind of burn; we burn with ultimate bodhicitta. When we feel the suffering of beings, this burns with a fire that demands action. It demands our own action in terms of practice, and it may demand action in the world as well. The greater this fire is, the greater that it is evident how one must proceed, even if it seems inconceivable that this chosen path could possibly work.

Ultimate bodhicitta usually comes about gradually, but it can come about all at once. How wonderful it would be to have a life filled with bodhicitta, instead of one shaped by competition and acquisition. Ultimate bodhicitta brings us to an empathy that is profound and deep, an empathy that encompasses everything and everyone and knows what to do and how to act in the moment. This is what ultimate bodhicitta is, this is what wisdom-exaltation is, this is what sublime activities are.

My way of cultivating ultimate bodhicitta is to practice tonglen and to practice it in all circumstances. Tonglen includes having a feeling of being able to take in all the pain in the world and rest in it. Or if that is too much, to rest in a little bit of pain. At first it may seem that taking in the pain of others couldn't possibly work, but it does.

No matter what appears, ultimate bodhicitta is the answer for you, for me, for us. When something that is upsetting or nerve-racking occurs, the energy of the upset is the resting place. The upset isn't a place to get away from; it's a place in which to rest profoundly and deeply, and in that profound rest, our view changes. All wisdom comes from direct insight due to a clarity that is the ultimate luminosity of our true mind. It's not anything scary and is not a cut-off place. Right here, right now, everything is clear-light luminosity.

❀

When we are dedicated to the practice of the teachings, our confusion slowly becomes clarified, in that the "confusion" is realized to be sublime wisdom and wisdom-exaltation. Life becomes a celebration, one which will allow us to reach the end of our lives without regret. No matter where you are, you are. It doesn't matter what's going on in your life, you are perfect as you are. No matter what appears, wisdom accommodates it, beyond anything known currently.

Just because you're going crazy and someone else is in a peaceful state, you don't need to compare yourself. Comparison and competition are ideas that are perpetuated by binary thinking, namely, that we have to position ourselves to our advantage. It's like, "I'm going to compete with you to be the best practitioner here," but competition in this way brings us nothing but dissatisfaction.

Another subtle way that we become angry and irritated is that we try to elevate ourselves above others, rather than finding a commonality. Binary thinking produces the idea that, "I would rather be right than happy." Competition results in: "I would rather be superior than happy." Even if in my distant past I chose some of the time to be right rather than happy, now I will always choose happiness! I know now that I am responsible for my own data and thereby my own happiness, and that I have a choice.

❀

We're each very unique. In our practice we're unique in a certain sense, and there are no two people who share exactly the same experience of anything. We have a commonality and a similarity, but each of us is experiencing a pattern—a karmic circumstance—that is unique to us. And yet, we're all in this together. The bottom line is that these patterns eventually reveal themselves as radiance, but not if we refuse to practice.

Even though these exalted qualities and activities are innate and are our true identity, there's nevertheless a period of becoming familiar with these qualities. The initial teachings give us a clear understanding of who we are. These are very profound teachings, and in their realization we are in a position of no more learning.

"No more learning" is the complete release from old ideas about the need to accumulate knowledge. It is the recognition that our true knowledge is vast and far beyond what we can presently know through binary thinking. In no-more-learning, the most novel and unexpected ideas can appear, ideas way beyond what anyone would have through binary thinking. These are ideas that have not been available to us before, and not only one idea, but endless ideas, and also ways of carrying them out to benefit beings.

THE UNDER-MUTTER

CHAPTER SIX

We practice, and we find a place within ourselves where there is nothing going on. No longer need we worry about having emotional upheavals with extreme ups and downs. We are no longer looking for relief from negative states or hoping for only positive states.

The conclusion that we are a separate self—and then a life lived through that conclusion—leads to a deep-seated and underlying pain. There may be a heaviness of feeling and a lethargy present for us that we can't get rid of, and we can find no binary/causal mechanism that can overcome it. In fact, many of the conventional methods that are supposed to soothe the mind don't soothe it at all. Causal mechanisms can't fully resolve these disturbances, but we can be put in touch with our own vulnerability, and through that, the yearning to be free of these things.

We feel trapped to some degree in these patterns we have developed for ourselves, and we sense that something is driving us that we can't quite identify. Well, let's identify it here. It could be called the "under-mutter." There is the "mutter" that we can identify and speak to and from, and then there is the "under-mutter," the things that are hidden from us. We know that something is there, but not exactly what it is. When we are immersed in the under-mutter, there are certain hidden things stewing in us, and they require a reckoning.

The under-mutter could be equated with the deep unconscious, the aspects of ourselves that aren't directly available to our surface cognition. The things that come up in the under-mutter can be very scary. Often the things that frighten us are part of the under-mutter, and the fear may suddenly arise, but we can't say exactly why or from where.

In the under-mutter are the most primitive anxieties, tensions and impulses that drive a person to do whatever they do. A hidden pattern has been established through the years that rises up and influences the conscious mind. The roots of the under-mutter go very deep. Even things that happened to us when we were preverbal have been stored in us. Then, of course, along the way in life we are accumulating thousands of experiences, and these also go into making up the under-mutter.

For each person the under-mutter is significant, and it is not easy to deal with; however, it's these things that are hidden from us that we need to come to terms with in order to be at peace. We each have had a different kind of life, and the under-mutter is whatever it is for each one of us, and it doesn't have the same basis or expression for everyone. Despite this somewhat ominous description, its origin and basis is the same beneficial energy that is present in each one of us.

⊛∞⊛

Courage is required to enable us to loosen up this profound under-mutter so that it can be clearly seen. With practice, sincerity, perseverance and skillful support, it can be clearly seen. We need to reach the point where we can rest deeply with the under-mutter and let everything be *as it is*. Once the under-mutter becomes apparent in its essence as open intelligence, and once it is rested with, it can be spontaneously released in each short moment. We will no longer be blindsided.

If, however, the under-mutter remains rooted in us, often a kind of obsessive thinking about things stays on and won't go away. There is a sort of speedy energy that rushes towards things and circumstances in order to describe them, and then we reflect these descriptions onto ourselves and others. This speedy energy ends up being reflected onto our entire environment.

We know how we feel when we attach these binary ideas to everything—good and bad, reward and punishment, right and wrong and so forth. When we believe in these binary ideas, we have a lot of speedy energy that names everything and makes us feel like we have to choose one oppositional pole or the other. With the rush into causal thinking and the drive to label and describe our experience, we may feel taken over by this speedy energy, and when we are, we don't feel comfortable.

However, when we rest as the energy of that speediness, rather than being hijacked by this causal thinking, the energy resolves into its primordial essence. When we rest as the pure energy of what we are, the tension and speediness are resolved. Our energy is always soft and warm. When we practice, simply resting as the softness and warmth in a direct way, rather than riding on the speedy energy, we are opened to a new way of seeing things. The protective barriers that we have used to protect ourselves are no longer needed.

🔔

It is so helpful to remember that no matter the intensity of the speedy energy, we are never separated from the heart essence. The warmth and softness of what we really are is what we rest as, rather than trying to herd ourselves into some special kind of idea. All the energies of the body and mind are simply the energies of the heart essence itself. The heart essence is infinite, inexhaustible, unstoppable, indestructible and ineffable, so there is nothing to be done.

By practicing with the heart essence at the forefront, we feel happiness. This happiness can be carried forth in our lives so that others can be touched with happiness. When we rest in this very simple way, we become completely familiar with the basis of love and happiness, and then it naturally touches others.

By resting with speedy energy, so that it no longer informs our thought process, we realize that we're not a limited character. We become an expression of the loving energy that we have discovered in ourselves, and we no longer aggress upon ourselves or anyone else.

This loving energy is our own reality, always has been, is now and will always be. There was nothing to go to in the past, there's nothing to go to in the future and there's no need to even decide about what's now. When we rest as our soft warmheartedness, it becomes very easy for everything to resolve.

✿

So, with that confidence, let's look into something that has possibly held sway over us for a long time, for example, anxiety. Things have come up that made us feel anxious, things that seemed that they were uncontrollable and would never go away. When we rest as the anxiety, rather than being taken over by it, we now have a choice we did not have before.

Maybe in the past we would have only listened to the sound that named the energy as "anxiety" and would have been pulled along by that definition. But now we can allow that named sound to dissipate into the sound of sound. We had learned to go in lockstep according to causal reasoning and to see everything as a product of cause and effect, but now we rest; we let things be as they truly are, and we treat ourselves with warmth and affection.

If we feel trapped in an idea or we feel unable to find a way to continue on in our lives, it is important to simply rest until the path forward becomes clear. When we rest, the path forward does become clear, but this doesn't mean that the path will necessarily be the one that we expected to take! We rest, and we proceed compassionately. We entertain every possibility; we invite it in and let it be *as it is*. We rest and respond to the ebb and flow of life in all its many forms.

46

Impermanence is always a crucial factor in whichever path we take. Never to forget: impermanence, impermanence, impermanence. Everything that we have hoped for is changeable and temporary. That's the reality of it.

There is likely no greater motivation than being able to see how much of life has been a disappointment. So then, if all our previous disappointments are flooding over us, what a great incentive to practice that can be. By being upfront and clear about impermanence and disappointment, we become more familiar with workability. We find ways to make life with all of its twists and turns workable.

The term "workability" points to flexibility, openness and skillfulness, but also playfulness and good humor. This is a sign of accomplishment: playfulness and good humor. It isn't something that has been cooked up or contrived. There is a joy and a zest for life, and the light of wisdom and compassion are present, regardless of what is occurring. This is where workability is to be found.

We need to have faith, and we have to also have trust and devotion. Those are the three: faith, trust and devotion. Faith and trust are needed for devotion. Building faith and trust is necessary, and one of the best ways to build faith is through practice.

We practice, and we find a place within ourselves where there is nothing going on. No longer do we need to worry about having emotional upheavals with extreme ups and downs. We are not looking for relief from negative states or hoping for only positive states. If this possibility is available to everyone, and yet we think that we are not worthy enough to receive it, that wouldn't make much sense, would it?

❈

I feel so grateful for having the bountiful life that I have, but I know that the circumstances of my life are impermanent. No matter where I live and no matter how much I love where I live and what I have, it will pass away, and I will too. How do we best come to terms with all of this? That's the question we're attempting to answer in the whole of this book.

We can see that our own journey is complicated and demanding, as are the lives of others. Yet, we grow confident in our ability to entertain the diversity of demands in the world and to respond to them skillfully—demands such as aging and death.

And for me, well, I'm old! I don't feel old; I feel younger than I ever have, but most people would consider me to be old. Be that as it may, I feel more like I'm thirty-five. But when I was actually thirty-five, it was a confusing time for me. I felt messed up, believe me, especially after drinking a couple of bottles of vodka a day for a while.

I certainly don't do that anymore, but I am so grateful that I had the experience. Indeed, as I said earlier, how beneficial it is when our disappointments wash over us and we are able to find the motivation within ourselves to inquire deeply. I'm not going to marginalize myself because this happened, nor do I have to keep it from anyone. We have the disappointing and challenging experiences we have in life, and that's just the way it is. Whatever they are, they relate to our unfoldment as the brilliant, exalted beings we are.

THE MOONLIGHT SHINING IN COUNTLESS PONDS

CHAPTER SEVEN

Whatever our experience is, it is like moonlight shining in countless ponds. Moonlight doesn't have a little bit here and a lot there; it shines in all ponds equally. What is right here and right now shines perfectly. It is not a split off shine. It is the shine here, regardless of where we have interpreted "here" to be.

Due to the inherited beliefs of our culture, developed over centuries, many people believe that they were born a mistake and that they are somehow inherently sinful and unworthy. This belief can be very, very subtle and yet play such a dominant role in the way a society expresses itself. This notion that we are a mistake is a very powerful one, and if we believe that we are a mistake, we will likely see that assumption frequently proven to us. We may rely on others to prove it to us, and if we can't find anyone else to prove it to us, then we'll prove it to ourselves.

It is not difficult to see the painful depths of the suffering that people are experiencing, but please don't despair! No matter what arises, don't despair, because you have the power to not despair. When despair arises, it is there because it has been named "despair." When we give a name like this to our energy of sublime qualities and activities and then ride on that horse, we don't feel well. We feel more and more desperate, but this need not be the choice we make.

Maybe even now as you read this you feel terrible and you don't know what to do. This is where the power of the practice can come into full evidence. As you rest with all of what is arising in you and you let it be *as it is*, you might have realizations that are new to you, recognitions you have never had before. You might even be tempted to gradually give up the old way of thinking that led to your misery! What a courageous act that would be: to leave the familiarity and security of what you have known before and to be open to what you don't yet know.

With this courageous intention, you are in a position to make things workable. Everything is workable, no matter what it is. If something comes up that you feel you can't handle, remember this key point: it is workable. Even in the depths of despair, there is something in you that is completely untouched by despair, and it is workable.

Each named thought or emotion releases spontaneously. So, what does that tell us? We all have these energies come up, but they release, and instead of being mastered by them, we can rest with them. That's how the afflictive energy dissipates. In that resolution, clear seeing becomes available to us, and we see the light of everything, the sound of everything, and we know that this is what we are: the light and the sound and the dynamic energy of everything.

❧❧❧

The philosopher Herbert Spencer once said, "There is a principle which is proof against all arguments and which cannot fail to keep a man in everlasting ignorance. That principle is contempt prior to investigation." How could we be so arrogant as to assume that we have the only way of thinking—binary, causal, rationalistic thinking—and that this is the only possibility?

It's always better to have the greatest context possible to look at things, one that is simple, but not overly simple. Letting things be as they are, resting as awareness for short moments many times, being vulnerable and open to what we don't already know, seeing that things are workable—that is a simple method, but not overly simple.

There are many ways of understanding things and not just the ways that we hear about in schools and universities or which were passed on to us by our culture. Privileged people have had sovereignty over knowledge through educational, religious and economic institutions that have great power in the world. Down through time, established wealth, governments and organizations have defined what knowledge is and what it is not, and defined what is possible and what is not.

Through this, we have had a sort of logic based on binary thinking that has been educated into us over many years that has determined how we describe the world we see. However, the way we have learned to describe the world doesn't describe it accurately. We have learned only one perspective, one that is based on cause and effect and which has a purely rationalistic perspective from which we relate to our experience.

We have seen the events in our experience as either positive or negative, and this distorted perspective shaped the way we live. And yet, the mind can be devoted to another kind of energy; that is, it can become susceptible to another kind of intelligence. Absolutely everything we know or learn is an aspect of and a representation of a great intelligence—an open intelligence—and we can be introduced to this greater intelligence and see that there is something far beyond mere rationality and the binary/causal thinking in which we have been educated.

The world's major religions and educational institutions barely touch on this sublime knowledge, but through inquiry and practice we can gain familiarity with it. There may be only a very few fortunate people who ever have some sense that there is something greater in life than their conventional inherited knowledge. For these fortunate ones, "a greater intelligence" is not only a vague idea they have heard somewhere. They have the unique opportunity to recognize and decisively realize this intelligence for what it is.

"Know thyself," has been a maxim in Western culture for more than 2,500 years. However, in the West we have learned to approach things materially, meaning that it is in material things that we will find satisfaction. "Material" also includes all of our thoughts, feelings, sensations, experiences, aspirations and so on that we take to be substantial and independently existing things. When we find out that the material realm will not bring us ultimate satisfaction, this insight can be very disruptive to our previously held assumptions!

In maintaining our practice, there need be no ambition for achieving a goal or gaining some material advantage as a consequence of action. There isn't, "Oh, I'm going to devote myself to practice so I can get more money, more satisfaction and a better life circumstance and then maybe also become enlightened." Those situations may come about, but this is not a goal of practice. Material things that are achieved are related to ordinary power to get things done, but the greatest "acquisition" is the peace, bliss and love of open intelligence which we have had all along.

The practice is short moments many times. In a short moment we bring radiant awareness to an event or perception. It doesn't mean having one fixed idea, for example, something that is going to be "The Idea." Wisdom doesn't hold to a fixed opinion. It involves seeing clearly without impediment. It is knowing what to do and how to act in all situations.

I feel that the recognition of open intelligence will become more and more important due to the crises we have in the world. People want to be strong and capable, but there haven't been methods that give people total confidence to do what they feel is necessary.

Human beings are going to need to practice this greater intelligence. This will be the intelligence that will be recognized and utilized in the future, and this recognition is increasingly coming about, and it will continue to come about. The rain comes down one drop at a time and it fills a large container one drop at a time. Similarly, in one short moment at a time this greater intelligence will be revealed to a thirsting world.

Wisdom lets us rest in clarity and then adjust easily as we go along. Everything is always changing, so how could we make a specific plan that would meet all the infinite nuances that are possible? Everything needs to be responded to as it comes. Even when we do plan, we can't count on things going according to that plan. We show up, and whatever needs to be done in the moment, that is what is done.

Then, the other part of that statement is that nothing is actually ever fully done or finished. If we perform some action with a goal in mind, we really can't expect that goal to be fully reached. All is changing and impermanent and there is no end to the flow of things. There is always more to do, and then we die!

There really isn't a final destination called "realization" or "enlightenment." Realization isn't a reward we're getting through practice. That we actually have no goal is a very advanced realization! How could we possibly have an expected goal when, whatever the goal is, the outcome won't be the one we have envisioned? There is just the ceaseless unfolding.

We simply are expressing who we are, resting without effort and allowing our actions to come from the easy place. It doesn't mean that life itself will be easy, because we never know what tragedy awaits us. However, in the face of whatever comes our way, more and more we make our life easeful and effortless. There is gentleness in our lives rather than fear and aggression.

Whatever our experience is, it is like moonlight shining in countless ponds. Moonlight doesn't have a little bit here and a lot there; it shines in all ponds equally. What is right here and right now shines perfectly. It is not a split off shine. It is the shine here, regardless of where we have interpreted "here" to be.

TO GO TO ANY LENGTHS IN PRACTICE

CHAPTER EIGHT

Our commitment must be to go to any lengths. I am aware of the defenses and resistances in myself and in others, and so the importance of practice is very clear to me. I keep showing up for practice because I love to! I feel undeterred now.

It is really important that we are aware when we are becoming very reactive, because if we are taken over by extreme reactivity, we could cause harm to ourselves and others. Whenever we feel very reactive, it's about us. It's not about whom or what we are reacting to; it's about us. Everything is rooted in our own perception.

In our culture, to a large degree our vantage has been turned to the externalized world. Instead of turning to our true selves, we have been trained to look outside for happiness and also to think that we need to get rid of or avoid the things that bother us. The idea that anything needs to be eradicated is an idea that should be challenged. It's very important to practice short moments and to ask for support. "What is this about? Why do I feel so strongly about this?"

The only place we can truly feel empowered is in ourselves, because that is where the transcendent solution is. This transcendent solution comes from the autonomy and agency that we all have in our human life. It is a total misconception to think that we're going to receive autonomy and agency from some source outside ourselves.

Through self-disclosure and candor and through knowing oneself thoroughly, we come to understand what the energies within us actually are and how they have been misinterpreted and mislabeled. I know for sure what the resistance and defenses in us are: they are the energy of sublime wisdom!

❦

We each have our own viewpoints in life, and I am committed to respecting other people's viewpoints. How do I know whether I'm respecting other people's viewpoints or not? I know by the way that I respond. It's so easy to gauge, because a genuine response from the authentic self is humble, vulnerable and filled with beneficial intent. It is free of complaint and reaction and of any need to defend or defeat. Because of my practice, I have faith in myself to handle things and to keep showing up skillfully, regardless of what is occurring.

If there are others who don't agree with us, what is the solution? Is it to say, "They're wrong and I'm right."? No. Instead, we have a connection with them based on full relationship. We show up in vulnerability and we allow our resistance and defenses to rest. In doing so, the resistance and defenses self-release, and there's only more vulnerability. The first moment we practice vulnerability we are making the situation workable, and then more and more it becomes workable. This workability becomes the space of our life, so that we can greet everything in a skillful way.

Realization is absolute vulnerability. Absolute vulnerability equals compassion. There's no way to have self-compassion without complete vulnerability. There's no way to have compassion for others unless we address our compassion for ourselves.

We have to have enough intimacy with ourselves to be vulnerable, and maybe through that vulnerability we can allow everything to be *as it is*, and we can then truly show up in our relationships. We know that, no matter what someone else is expressing or feeling, we can remain whole, complete,

56

empowered and totally in the here and now. We settle into our natural intelligence, and the more we live from that vantage, the more we know how to skillfully respond in each moment.

I feel that in truly meeting ourselves and others at the most fundamental level, we are able to see what our natural urge for life is. Most of us don't know what "our natural urge for life" means, because we have for so long relied on binary thinking that is blind to the true essence of things. Due to that way of being, certain conduct has flowed forth in us, like for instance the afflictive reactivity spoken about earlier.

We have suffered and caused others to suffer, but now we don't want to suffer any longer. We want to feel whole, harmonious and at peace, but maybe we didn't know that even in the midst of suffering we can feel harmonious and at peace! We've been trying to run away from suffering and to escape it at any cost. When we hear in the teachings that there is an end to suffering, we might think, "Oh good, my suffering is going to end and I'm going to feel great and I'm going to be enlightened."

We imagine ourselves jumping from what we consider "bad" over to what we think is "good." However, when we rest within the suffering itself, that's when we find wisdom. For instance, for me, I had thought that vulnerability was an intense form of suffering, and I did not want to be vulnerable. Yet, through practice I found that vulnerability is a path beyond suffering.

People are not going to be able to avoid vulnerability any longer! We have already seen in the pandemic that everyone all over the world has been forced to face their vulnerability. I find this fantastic. I don't find Covid fantastic, but I find the coming together in the shared experience and shared vulnerability fantastic.

With any of the binary opposites—good and bad, happy or sad—it's possible in any situation to hold both appraisals as equal and even in open intelligence. This is what it means to be impartial: to hold both as equal and even. It is also so that we don't need to have either one or the other to feel whole, because we feel whole in ourselves regardless of the binary descriptions.

No matter what happens, there really isn't an agenda to follow, and more and more we see that no one ever did anything! Everything is happening spontaneously. We may "do" something, like say, I may write a teaching and it may be useful, but to claim personal authorship is an illusion.

There are many apparently unintelligible statements like this that defy all ideas about cause and effect!

✿

If we just think about it, we as an individual identity are not doing anything to make the body work. We can do things that make the body work better, but the body is a self-regulating energetic process that does not need our guidance or approval.

When we rest, we're simply getting involved in what our energy is, rather than what it isn't. What it *isn't* is oppositional thinking. We allow everything to be *as it is* and know that we will know everything that is needed in the moment in order to take skillful action. We also see that all action taken will be taken to further guarantee the integration of this way of intelligence into human life.

This is what I am charged to do by the Dzogchen lineage of gurus: I want to further guarantee the integration of this way of intelligence into human life, and I have committed myself to being devoted to the enlightenment of all beings immediately. That's my intention every single day, and I have no other intention.

We learn in the West that our mind is up in the head; however, our mind is in our entire body—and everywhere else, for that matter! Everything is mind. If we use the energy of our mind to obsess over something, we are severely limiting the immense possibilities of the mind. We can be taken over by obsessive thinking; however, that obsessiveness can be set free in vulnerability. The solution is more vulnerability—not less—to the energies in our body.

Our bodily energies tell us everything about how life is unfolding. For example, maybe something isn't going right with the people we're in relationship with. In an intimate relationship so many things can come up that we don't want to see, don't want to feel and which we just want to go away. However, it is up to each of us in that situation to be responsible for ourselves and our reactions. We can be responsible for ourselves by resting, being vulnerable and open and appropriately expressing what is needed to foster a beneficial relationship.

❈

Practice is so very important in my life. I would go to any lengths to be able to practice, any lengths. Our specific motivation leads us to practice in the way that we do to the extent that we do. The motivational energies lead us to a certain pattern of practice, and that is how we ended up here with this very precious gift of a practice that exalts us in every single instant.

Our commitment must be to go to any lengths. I am aware of the defenses and resistances in myself and in others, and so the importance of practice is very clear to me. I keep showing up for practice because I love to! I feel undeterred now. In my younger life I thought my thoughts, feelings, sensations, emotions and so forth constituted life, and because I had been holding onto the thoughts and emotions, I was actively practicing being deterred! I thought that the dictionary definition of these thoughts and emotions constituted human life. But of course, that was not correct.

Whenever there's some kind of enormous upset in my life, I know there's something brilliant coming along. I know there's something where I need to make a big change, and whatever the event was, it somehow was needed for that change to take place in terms of my intention and commitment.

I was very fortunate to have been exposed to things that could really help me—things that, seen from a conventional point of view, were very threatening and saddening. I really don't think I would have the joyful life I have now if I hadn't been introduced to them. With whatever suffering appears in my life now, the distinction is that I don't act any longer from the belief that suffering must be avoided.

If you're suffering, please know that I understand, and that I have suffered, too. Again, for me suffering is wisdom. When we want to run away from our afflictive emotions, that is the time when we need to stay fixed and stalwart, because that is when we'll find what we're looking for. Instead of running away from, we run towards!

Section Two:

EDUCATING AND SUSTAINING OURSELVES

9. The Reality of Who We Are   62

10. Wisdom-Exaltation and Sublime Activities   68

11. Self-Compassion   74

12. A Feast of Delight   80

13. Our Genuine Self   86

14. We Know That We Don't Know!   92

15. Peaceful Mind   97

16. The Wisdom of Discernment   103

THE REALITY OF WHO WE ARE
CHAPTER NINE

When we are first introduced to the resting practice, we are introduced to the reality of who we are, and if we are fortunate, we can no longer escape it!

No matter what appears in our daily experience, it can be rested with. To the conventional mind, an extremely negative thing may not seem like something we can rest with, but we do in fact have that capacity. The appearance might not be one we wished for and one which is very disruptive, but there is not a single thing that appears that is not rest-able. The power of resting becomes more apparent through ongoing, persistent and devoted practice.

With some discernment, we can see that no matter what appears in our mind, it arises, abides and subsides. A thought arises, abides and subsides, and then another separate thought, arising, abiding, subsiding, and then another, and another. If we can rest with clarity and alert intention, we can see that multiple thoughts are arising, but not as a continuous connected chain.

Each thought that appears then releases. It doesn't exist permanently, and we can see that whatever appears in our mind will subside and will not appear in exactly the same way again. How could we possibly posit that all these disparate thoughts put together actually constitute something substantial? We really can't. We can only really count on impermanence. Everything is always in process, and there is nothing that can be solidified or perpetuated. All things are impermanent and nothing can be held on to.

If we only pay attention to what is going on in the mind, we become fixed into what the mind is perpetually focusing on. We become ordinary, which means that we have neglected our exalted nature and we are existing only within the narrow scope of our ordinary thoughts and emotions.

We already have everything we need to be present for our resting practice. By simply investigating the mind, we gain a vantage on life that we could never have had before. When we fully connect with ourselves in this subtle and sublime way, we grow in our compassion for this suffering world. As practitioners, each one of us has our own glorious garden of wisdom and ways to serve. Each moment of practice can unify us with others in compassionate embrace.

❦

When we are first introduced to the resting practice, we are introduced to the reality of who we are, and if we are fortunate, we can no longer escape it. Maybe we have tried before to understand the reality of who we are and were not able to do so, and yet upon full introduction, we are on the road to understanding. We may not grasp it fully in the beginning, but we gain the conviction that, if we practice what we've been introduced to for short moments many times, we will grow in a sense of our own enrichment, and we can no longer avoid being who we truly are.

The emphasis for most of us growing up was on what we have learned to call "thoughts and emotions" and that these thoughts and emotions have the power to control us and dictate our thinking and behavior. Many of us have been looking for emotional resilience throughout our lives, and the resilience that has been sought after comes not through indulging or avoiding emotions, but through resting with the emotions. Emotional resilience is not to be found in arranging our inner and outer circumstances into something entirely positive.

No person, no event, no accomplishment, no wealth can give us the emotional strength and resilience that practice can give us.

The glory of these teachings is that we can learn how to transform emotional energy into wisdom. Whatever the emotional energy is or how it is described, in its essence it is wisdom. What a gift it is to be able to take that emotional energy that so upset us and now have it available to us as wisdom-energy. So, to cash in on this gift, we must practice. The instruction then is to keep practicing regardless of what happens. Keep practicing, keep practicing, keep practicing.

We're always generating our own reality, whether that reality is based on reified and binary thinking or on wisdom-insight. When we let things be as they are, gradually our view becomes more transparent. However, sometimes the idea comes that we don't have enough strength to go on in practice, and we think, "Oh, I just can't do it." This doubt is something else to let be *as it is*. When we do not let everything be *as it is*, we're really letting ourselves down.

We need to build up our practice bank account! This "bank account" is not dollars and cents, but wise activity and compassion. Wise, because it is spontaneous and beneficial and because it is coming from our authentic nature.

Everyone is vested with the authentic self and no one is left out, even if at times we feel that we are unworthy. But, you see, thinking that everyone else would be qualified to discover the authentic self but we wouldn't be is a sort of reverse arrogance. We're each as qualified as anyone else, because we are not attaining something new, but only discovering what is already present. With practice we come to see what is possible.

Practice is only about *right now*. We're not headed for a place or a state that exists somewhere else. Who we are is only here and now and will only ever be here and now. That is true for all of us. Everyone can practice.

So much comes up that could take us out of our practice, and there are times when it seems impossible, or it seems like there can't be any benefit to be gained from it. Never mind, keep practicing. We are eventually able to integrate practice into all of our life, and because we do so, we have the realizations that come from continued practice. One way of thinking about it is that in every short moment we are strengthening the power of wisdom.

A true introduction to an extraordinary teaching comes when there is a genuine and transmissive communication between two people: the teacher and someone who is open to instruction. We meet another human being just like us and we think, "Hmm, is what was possible for them possible for me?" For many of us, it may be the first authentic introduction to a wisdom teaching.

We can feel the love present in the encounter with the teacher, but it could be that we're scared of them or we don't understand what is going on or we're completely overwhelmed. However, we're there because there is something in us that has drawn us to that person and that particular situation.

We have been attracted in this way and feel such an intense connection, even if we only go once. We have been introduced, no matter what else we may think about it, and we will recall it on our deathbed, even though this recall has nothing to do with memory. When we hear the truth, we know it and it connects with us. We carry it with us.

In terms of my own practice, well, I keep it so very, very simple. I practice guru devotion. That's it, and I don't have another practice. I have done many practices in the past, but guru devotion is my practice now. Why is it my practice? Because I was told it was the quickest way to enlightenment. What is more, I was completely undone the first time I met the great Tibetan gurus, Wangdor Rimpoche and Minling Trichen Rinpoche.

There was no way to keep up the mental activity I had going on in my head, and it came to a halt when I met them. I had a clear notion that I was in the right place, because I had never felt that way in my entire life. I knew then that they held a way of life that undid me and brought me to tears of incredible joy—the joy of knowing that we can be human in the most exalted way possible. In practicing short moments, we become more aware of ourselves as we truly are, and we become more aware of the rich resources that are already our own.

✿

The qualities of human exaltedness have never been needed more for us as individuals and for us as a civilization. We want to be able to meet the anxieties and challenges of today and in the future. We want to know what to do when we feel stressed, tired, angry or lonely, and we want to know how to make sense of things we see going on around us. We want to be part of the solution that will bring comfort to ourselves and to a suffering world.

There has never been a time like this before in the world, so we are very blessed to be here with the practice and to be able to face this unknowable future. Whether it's a good future or a bad one, we can make it workable through bringing practice to it.

When we are truly attuned to ourselves, we cannot help but be compassionate. When we're in touch with our own pain and suffering, it becomes easier to feel the suffering of others. I know for certain that in practice we become more compassionate. We can see this compassion, this bodhicitta, manifesting in ourselves, and we can see it manifesting in other practitioners who have also attuned themselves.

Everything that I have been taught and experienced in my life has been valuable to me. Whether it was hurtful at the time or whether it was great, it's all gold to me now. The more that I was open to what I was being taught through those experiences, the more present and available I became, and the more I knew that I don't know anything at all, and the more I could see that everything is *as it is*, united and indivisible.

No reason to be delighted by a wonderful life or dragged down by a not-wonderful life. Wonderful life, not-wonderful life—it's all transformative if it is allowed to transform. We are very blessed to be able to be magicians within our own minds!

WISDOM-EXALTATION AND SUBLIME ACTIVITIES

CHAPTER TEN

When we come to realize that we are exalted and that we have within us the power for sublime activities unlike anything we've ever carried out before, a whole new world opens up for us. We become familiar with a way of perceiving life that is native to us, but that we've never known about.

Many of us are not yet alert and alive to our feeling energy. By "feeling energy" I don't mean only thoughts or emotions. I mean the actual fundamental energy that gives us wisdom-exaltation and creates sublime activities. The wisdom-exaltation and sublime activities are found in the energy from which the emotions come, especially the emotions that cause us the most pain.

Please pay attention to the energy in the body when you are having emotions. If you feel fear, for example, feel that energy in your body fully, but without the need to label it as you may have done in the past. What exactly is the energy in your body that you have identified as fear or anything else? This can also be practiced with the energies that have been named other things, such as jealousy, desire, shame, joy, arrogance or pride.

We have quite a menu there, along with hope, desire, anger, aggression and so many others. The thoughts and emotions are this natural feeling energy, but the energy has been mislabeled as "thoughts" and "emotions," while all the time remaining exactly *as it is* without alteration.

The resolution of anger is very important because it is the platform for the resolution of the other emotions. It's really important to get in touch with that slight urge to be angry and aggressive. That first inkling of anger might arise, but by identifying the energy in our body that has been described as that particular emotion, we're able to get a sense of what that energy actually is and bring awareness to it.

If you do not feel the energy in your body, turn on some music and dance around! Feel the energy of the music and feel the floor reverberating from the music and filling your body with that incredible energy.

⊛∞⊛

Engaging in aggression really limits our ability to practice. We'll stay stuck wherever we are if we continue to practice aggression. All aggressive movements in life begin with a single thought, and Dzogchen teaches that if that single thought is allowed to generate further, it could bring about a lot of pain for oneself and others. Initially, we may not be aware of this tendency towards aggression. However, more and more as we practice we become aware of it, and the more we are aware of it, the more we are horrified by our previous aggressive behavior. In this case, it's good to be horrified!

Please rest as aggression. It means resting as the aggression arises and not trying to get rid of it. Resting as the aggression is what is needed. When we rest as the aggression itself, we are able to recognize its illusory nature. An aggressive impulse could be, "I'm so mad at him and I'm going to make sure he knows it." With the first impulse of, "I'm so mad at him," that is the time to really rest into that thought.

If you can't become calm that way, bring the breath deep into the lungs and let it out slowly through your nose, and be intent on providing yourself with the resources from the practice of rest. That will bring calm and lessen the anger. We want to find the wisdom in aggression. When we foster aggression, it's difficult to find the wisdom, but if we experience aggression and we practice wisdom, that is a different approach. The aggressive energy is the wisdom of discernment, but we cannot know that unless we resolve aggression.

Resting as nonaggression we can meet each person with a nonaggressive attitude. I was surprised when I practiced this, because earlier in my life I had no idea that I was running with so much of this aggressive energy. I hadn't thought of myself as being that way, but I eventually noticed that when I was in situations where I didn't agree with what was going on or where someone was being harmed, I would have aggressive energy come up.

The very act of resting naturally is non-aggressive. We're not aggressing on ourselves and we're not aggressing on anyone else. I do want to say it again: please do not harbor aggression, because aggression removes what has been attained in practice. It really does, so this is a very important point.

♣

When we think we are the body that is doing something—a body that is born, lives and dies—we are only seeing a fragment that is based on a mental understanding, but that fragment becomes how we see ourselves and how we relate to all of life. However, in fact, we have a connection with everything, and that connection is not merely a fragmented mental idea.

We gain a sense of the intelligence that we already are, and we acknowledge it for short moments many times. This doesn't mean that we're trying to paste some other kind of positive label on the emotions that come up or avoid them or replace them with something better. That isn't it at all. It's a matter of becoming familiar with everything *as it is*. When we bring awareness to something, we're acknowledging that it is awareness and nothing else other than awareness.

With this practice of acknowledging the energy *as it is*, we come to find that we are increasingly alert, and we don't feel as tired or distracted as we might have before. We have abundant energy and we are not so easily moved by aggression any longer. The more we practice, the less agitation and aggression we experience.

When concerns come up, we rest *as* the concern. It doesn't mean we get *into* the concern; it means we're resting as the energy of the concern. The concerns come and then they go, and we might not even realize they've come, but then, *poof,* they've gone, because through practicing we have supported the capacity to rest as the concerns appear.

Instead of the emotions being troublesome energies—or really exciting ones—more and more we find that, no matter what the emotion is, it is seen for what it is. With rest, it resolves and spontaneously releases. The more we practice to the point of spontaneous release, the more emotions don't trouble us anymore. We see that the definitions we have had of emotions are not what emotions really are.

When we come to realize that we are exalted and that we have within us the power for sublime activities unlike anything we've ever carried out before, a whole new world opens up for us. We become familiar with a way of perceiving life that is native to us, but that we've never known about.

We enter a realm of joy. This joy is not any kind of a goal; it is more like an indication that one is on the right path. It is also not the form of temporary joy that comes and goes according to outer circumstances. This joy emerges naturally from our own brilliant and ever-present intelligence.

We do not want to be fragmentary practitioners of short moments—sometimes on, sometimes off, with no real devotion to the practice. If we are fragmentary practitioners, we get the result of fragmentary practice, but when we practice in a deep and profound way, we get a deep and profound result. When we see all of life in the most clarified manner, we begin to be a fierce practitioner. When we practice ongoingly, we develop the profound friendliness of unbearable compassion.

The teachings and practices are very simple and very direct, and when we practice as instructed, we obtain the benefit. As we go along, we experience a powerful expression of the teachings that is called "cutting through." It means cutting through all of our assumptions based on binary thinking and cause and effect. We all grow up with all kinds of ideas, but whatever the ideas may be, there's a way to cut through, and that is the short moments practice. Every single short moment is a skilled adjustment of the mind.

❈

One of the aspects of that skilled adjustment is an upsurge of bodhicitta, to the point of ultimate bodhicitta, which is unbearable compassion. What takes place is the emergence of a more comprehensive view. Ultimate bodhicitta comes about in a realization of complete humility. There is a feeling of being one hundred percent humbled and grateful to have access to a way of life that is so different from the brutality we now realize we were experiencing in our life of reification. There is a lot of brutality in the world, and sometimes it is very painful to acknowledge that brutality.

Ultimate bodhicitta draws on our realization of not only the suffering and pain in the world in general, but the very deep and abiding pain within ourselves. We have been trained up in so many ways that have caused us to suffer, and we have tried to avoid that suffering, but when we rest, we open up to everything. That is how we discover our authentic self: by opening up to everything and excluding nothing.

We're warm and direct in our service to the world without having to manufacture anything. We don't have to try to contrive compassion, because our compassion is based on innate bodhicitta and not on *trying* to practice compassion. When we proceed to ultimate bodhicitta, we deeply realize the complete suffering of all beings, including ourselves. We realize it so much that it brings us to tears. In that complete realization of suffering, the tremendous energy to carry out sublime activities begins to take place. Wisdom-exaltation and sublime activities come along with the realization of what is true in life.

There is the story that I have told so many times about a poor man who has gold buried under his small shack, but who does not know it. All of his life he has thought of himself as being totally poverty-stricken, but all the while the gold is there right beneath him, waiting to be discovered. I think that's a very beautiful metaphor, because in the same way, we have such great wealth within us that has lain there undiscovered.

When we take a short moment, we are acknowledging this wealth; we are acknowledging who we are. When we practice, we're getting to know the genuine self that is already fully accomplished. There is no getting to be gotten, no doing to be done. We are no longer trying to construct an individual identity.

In this practice, everyone is equally worthy to be who they are, because they are already who they are. We all are who we are, and we'll never be able to get away from it, no matter what we do. How could any of us be the only one left out of this majesty? We can never be free of freedom. Yes indeed, we can never be free of freedom! When we practice short moments, in each short moment we know what real freedom is, and as our understanding becomes so refined that we feel exalted, we know that our practice really has delivered a profound result.

SELF-COMPASSION

CHAPTER ELEVEN

We're born with self-compassion and compassion for others—ultimate bodhicitta and empathy. We are filled with these already, so we don't need to go anywhere to find them.

I want to focus here on self-empathy and self-compassion. Practicing tonglen—giving and receiving—is not only compassion for others, but also self-compassion. When we are practicing tonglen and we're giving and receiving, where is that occurring? It's occurring within us. We are resting in the energy within us.

When we begin to relate to the energy inside our body and we rest in that energy, we are then able to establish the teachings in ourselves in an entirely new way. We don't have to run around looking for self-compassion or trying to marshal it up. If, however, we find ourselves saying, "I just can't generate any self-compassion," that's a perfect opportunity for self-compassion.

In our interconnected global culture today, we can hear many people expressing their pain and suffering, so in that way there's no shortage of opportunity to practice giving and receiving. An urge to share ourselves with others comes about. In giving, receiving and sharing, it's essential to first really be present with ourselves; only then can we really be present with someone else in their suffering.

We may be confronted with a news story in which a mother is talking about not having any food or water for her baby, and the baby is on the verge of death. We want to truly take in the situation the mother and child are facing. We need to deeply think about these things and ask ourselves, "What is this really like? How are these people feeling?" If there is anything that we can possibly do to directly assist in that situation, then of course we do. But however it may be, we can genuinely feel their suffering.

We connect with others on this feeling level, where we're not only interpreting what others feel, but also acknowledging what we feel in response to others' suffering. When we fully see and take in the suffering of the mother with her baby, an energy will arise in us.

One choice is that we would want to push this energy away, because we can't stand to see or hear things like this. Another choice is one in which we can allow ourselves to feel the inequities involved in some having food and water and others not, and we can enter another kind of intelligence, an intelligence we haven't known before, even though it has always been within us.

◈◈◈

As we practice, we don't have to think about a goal, like say a goal of ultimate bodhicitta. Ultimate bodhicitta is already present, full-blown in everyone, and always fertile and growing. There's no limitation to this natural resource. We may already know what bodhicitta feels like within ourselves. If one were to contemplate a great compassionate being, that great being isn't doling out bodhicitta to us. Instead, a great being is showing us that we are non-different from them in having this naturally present bodhicitta.

Everyone is devotion-worthy. That's what it boils down to. However, if we only said, "Everyone is devotion-worthy," and left it at that, it might be difficult to take that statement in. But when we begin with self-compassion, then we really have a starting point for understanding what tonglen is. "If I am worthy of devotion and kindness, aren't others devotion-worthy as well?"

We not only connect with the incredible devotion and kindness within ourselves, but also with the great bliss that is the energy that constitutes both. If we are not usually kind to ourselves, we can just stop and rest, and we reconnect with who we really are.

We're an expression of the energy that is everywhere. We begin to really connect with the fact that everything, no matter what it is, is this vast energy, and it is offering us empathy, ultimate bodhicitta and relationship with itself. In this energy is everything about us and our presence and purpose in the world.

We don't even have to think about empathy; it's the energy in our body. When we rest in this energy, we come to know ourselves, and we come to love ourselves and feel confident in ourselves, and this naturally leads to the love of others.

In taking on the tonglen practice, think of the person who bugs you the most, then be with the person in the open embrace of empathy. There might be a person whom we hope to never see again, but then we do see them. Maybe we have great antipathy for them or we're even afraid of them. Instead of resistance or disdain, we can think, "Everyone suffers. I can surely be kind to this person, because I know my own pain, and through that, theirs."

So, let's go even further. Imagine the individual we hate the most, and despite that we can still rest and really connect with the energy that is in the other person. We can feel without impediment the energy that leads them to be the way they are. Instead of rejecting them, we offer our open hands, open hearts and warm, loving face. We don't have to feign a warm, loving face; it's the face of the great love that is already our own. This is a great, great gift to all of global humanity and our relation to all other beings.

If someone sees another person coming towards them with a warm and loving face, they may feel naturally drawn to connect with that person. They feel safe and that they can be with them easily. When we practice tonglen, we become warmer towards others, more generous, kind and easeful. Our living situation can be filled with joy, happiness and love wherever we go. We'll have empathy and compassion for ourselves and others that is very evident.

❦

In this practice we know that others are the same with us—same-same! We're not separate. "Global humanity" isn't just some sort of concept; global humanity is the energy that connects us with everything and everyone. There is no way to split up that energy.

We rest as the energy, and that rest gives us the disposition to give and receive, to share ourselves, to share empathy, to share compassion. In empathy we feel what the other person is feeling. This would include their feelings of being distraught and overwhelmed.

No matter how upset we feel, simply resting in the soothing energy in the body will transform these feelings into their great wisdom essence. Because we are resting in the energy in our body more and more, we're able to identify a great open space of love and bliss that is always-on.

�֍

We may have learned that "relationship" is a relationship with our family, friends, partners or others close to us, and we may struggle at times to happily be in relationships. The fact is that along the way we have not been supported to know ourselves in this simple way so that we can be in real relationship. When we are supported to know ourselves, we begin to see the fruits right away, and relationships can flourish. These relationships grow to include those who are outside our familiar circle.

Tonglen is essential in the caregiving of a child. Children have lots of emotions, and they go through all kinds of states. It is essential to really connect with a child on the level of their suffering, to really be with the suffering they feel, rather than trying to make it go away for them. We give them the assurance that we're fully there for them.

If we go to a child with an angry face, it doesn't make the child feel well. No matter what needs to be said to a child, we can say it with a warm, loving face. Even if we are disciplining the child, we are not required to put on an angry face. Instead, we're really feeling in our own heart what the child feels, and we would go to any lengths to serve the child.

We are entering fully into the life of the child. We are not just seeing the child as someone to manage, but truly developing a relationship with the child that is deep and complete. The child knows one hundred per cent that we're championing them. There is no greater gift to give a child, and no greater gift to give an adult.

ཨ།

We can practice tonglen with non-human beings as well. Maybe we have a dog or a cat; we can connect with the suffering of the dog or cat or any animal. How precious they are in their soft animal bodies! We can pat them, cuddle with them, love them. We're animals too, and we like having our soft animal bodies touched and to feel intimacy, warmth and love.

When we practice tonglen, we're relating our suffering to the suffering of everyone, instead of going with our common habit, which is to reflect only on our own suffering or maybe the suffering of our close loved ones. We come to feel much more at home in the world, and we are confident that we can face anyone and anything.

Through practicing tonglen, we come to feel at ease in situations where there may have been great fear and anxiety before. We're able to face situations that we would have avoided in the past. We can walk into a situation and possibly change the energy in it. We feel the energy in ourselves, and we rest in that energy and realize that there already is calming, soothing energy in the situation, and from this we speak and act.

A FEAST OF DELIGHT

CHAPTER TWELVE

This completeness is true for everyone, with no one left out. How could anyone be left out? Everyone is equally worthy and has access to the only power that really is.

A feast of delight. That's how I experience my life, even when circumstances are troubling, indeed, a feast of delight. In any life, there will be disturbing things going on that have to be met, but when we can meet them from a Dzogchen perspective, we're able to recognize the feast we have. There might be no food on the table and the wolf is at the door—which is not a circumstance we would have chosen for ourselves—but we nevertheless recognize the feast of delight that is available to us.

We have the wisdom to deal with things as they are. We're the master of the situation and are not mastered by it. When we are able to step up and greet each moment in its entirety, only then can we really understand the power of the practice. There is the luminosity, warmth and awe of emptiness, an "emptiness" that is not empty, because it's overflowing with luminosity. Luminous emptiness is not a place that is separate from everything else. It is inherent in all.

Another way to view emptiness is as accommodation and potential. Emptiness then means to accommodate and potentiate anything and everything, without anything becoming a "thing." The word "emptiness" can so easily be misunderstood as meaning a blank, void or nothingness, but it is entirely the opposite. Emptiness is the fullness of all things. As "accommodation and potential," the immense, all-embracing, infinitely powerful nature of emptiness is pointed to.

To have the perspective of emptiness means that at some point everything opens into luminosity. This is not conceptual and goes far beyond anything conceived by binary thinking.

All-pervasive and all-encompassing perfect love is ever available as that emptiness, that luminosity. We are never deprived. This isn't the way we were trained to think about things at all, so now we are training up in seeing ourselves as whole, beautiful and complete as we are. This completeness is true for everyone, with no one left out. How could anyone be left out? Everyone is equally worthy and has access to the only power that really is. From the very moment we are first introduced, the power and the riches are available.

❧❧

We learn in our practice how to deal with the binary ideas that we have used to describe who we are. We've taken on these binary and causal beliefs in the same way that we might take on a fashion fad! We see what the people around us are wearing, and we want what they have. In the same way we take on the beliefs of the culture around us. We want to be accepted—and not excluded—and so we take on the things that are acceptable to others. This process begins from the time we are very small.

But with the introduction to practice, something else unexpectedly happens. We are introduced to a way of being that feels very different from the binary-causal-rationalistic thinking that we have been involved with and that was so "fashionable" for us for so long. The introduction to open intelligence feels really satisfying and very freeing, and we want to establish what we have been introduced to more fully in our lives. We want this great feeling to be permanent within us, without realizing that it already is permanent within us! When we are introduced, we are merely seeing what has always been true about us all the way along.

We have to recognize our true self-value, no matter what we have taken ourselves to be in the past. We need to know that we have what it takes to recognize this reality, and the teachings reinforce us in this confidence. We feel more fully capable of answering the question: "What is the purpose of my life and how can I fulfill it?"

We have lived a life with thoughts, emotions and sensations as our driving force, because we have believed that these things form the basis of our lives. When we begin to question this and investigate it like a scientist would, we can pose the key questions, "Is this true? Is this who I really am? Am I relegated to this type of existence?" We come to see that there is something more in this existence that can nurture and support us and that can bring warmth into our hearts.

The role of the teacher and the teachings is to evoke what we already are. In that way, there is nothing to condemn or reject. When the feeling arises that we need to reject or even condemn something, that is a moment when we absolutely need to rest. If the habit of indulging, avoiding or rejecting our data is nourished, the tendency to do so will grow, in the same way that a plant grows when it is nourished. So too, our perception of the world as good and bad, acceptable and not-acceptable grows into fruition through nourishing that view.

When we practice, we do not have to contrive positive feelings about anything, and we don't have to combat negative ones either. We don't need to make the negative ones different, and we don't need to make the positive ones a source of desire. We don't have any way of keeping causal circumstances in place, so we're in a hopeless situation in that respect! Everything is subject to the law of impermanence.

In dealing with very afflictive past experiences, we don't want to try to repress or avoid them. The afflictive experience is present for us because it has been a part of who we have taken ourselves to be. It is not anything to get rid of or to denounce. The way to come to terms with it is to rest. We rest, and see beyond the mere description. We rest in the full presence of the affliction and thereby realize its luminosity and its emptiness. In the end it comes down to this.

※

We can think of the times where we might have been over the edge with conduct we really did not want to exhibit. We need to see what has motivated us in our most hideous moments in the past to act as we did. It is good for us to really consider when we have extended suffering to others rather than extending realization. The importance of the practice can become even clearer when things are considered in this way. It is obvious how very much suffering there is in us and in others in this world of ours.

Please be gentle with yourselves and with others. Please also consider yourselves already whole and with nothing to do, because this is the way it really is, regardless of how you have taken yourselves to be in the past. In speaking in this way, I'm speaking to who you really are, because I know that's all that you are. It isn't an option for me to think anything else, because I can't. Through my own practice I'm able to see you as you are, and I am unafraid to meet you fully.

There's the expression that "relationships are messy," and well, they are messy if we think they are messy and relate in the ways that keep them messy. Instead of gravitating towards the messy, we greet the moment *as it is*, and we rest with everything as it really is.

❈

In my long distant past, my usual ways of interacting with life on an intellectual basis didn't work, but through the embrace of the great Dzogchen gurus of Tibet, the recognition of the subtleties and nuances of the teachings occurred for me. I am humbled to the core to have ever been exposed to such beauty and elegance. This is the true elegance of who we are as human beings, and we can claim it fully. Why should we not claim our own birthright fully?

The communication of the teachings is very powerful, but the ineffable essence of the teachings is un-worded. Even if you don't yet understand the teachings intellectually, never mind. I have no need to understand them in that way. I'm interested in the teachings as a cure for what has afflicted us. I'm interested in them as a means to end suffering, not only for us as individuals, but also for us as a global community.

The great gurus stated clearly that short moments is the primary practice of Dzogchen. In short moments everything is already complete. We're not working to get somewhere else, like we probably have done all our lives—working towards something in order to reach a goal. There is no goal. We are complete in who we are right now, and we are never anything other than that.

Nothing is ever completely done or finished. Nothing. The idea that we're going to finish something or achieve a final goal is a cause of suffering. We're only right here and now. When we look at the past, present, future and causality—all these intellectual concepts that have so ruled us—we see that they're equal and even in their basis in open intelligence.

ཨ

In ancient times when the wisdom texts were written down, most people generally didn't travel more than a few miles from their homes. With better transportation it became easier for people to move around and communicate with each other. As more and more people were traveling and encountering other cultures, in many cases there was an acceptance of what might not have been accepted before.

In Tibet in ancient times the teachings needed to be communicated in a certain way, but in our times another type of communication is required. We need to honor who we are now as a global culture. Human beings exist now as an interconnected community, and as a result, the communication of the teachings is done in a way that is suitable to a modern and interconnected world, which is in some ways unlike the manner in which it was done in the past.

We compassionately extend to others what has been gifted to us. We send them love, kindness, understanding and empathy, and take in their pain. This is tonglen, and it is such a very powerful practice. I feel that tonglen is going to be very important to the future of the human race and to the preservation of life. We become willing to see all beings as precious—all beings, the ones we are close to and whom we cherish, and the ones who seem distant from us. All are embraced.

Our Genuine Self

CHAPTER THIRTEEN

The purpose of the teachings is to discover the genuine self. The genuine self, unlike the inauthentic self we have been trained in, is entirely spontaneous and cannot be held back. A genuine person spontaneously acts in accordance with who they actually are, rather than as who they are not.

For many, many years human beings, like you and I, have followed these wisdom practices. The reason we have the teachings in this modern era is that in each generation people were heart-moved by what they had received from their teachers, and out of their benevolence and generosity they made certain that the next generation had access to the teachings. They also provided us insights from their own experience with the teachings.

However, all over the world people have been trained to see only through the eyes of reified and binary thinking. When this is all we know, we invariably develop a false identity, a false self. When we take ourselves to be our false, conditioned self, we cannot see the real world, and we don't actually know what it is.

Particularly in the Western countries, and of course elsewhere as well, we're taught to try to get rid of faults and become virtuous. But as we dive deeper into our practice, we inch into a space of being okay with who we are. This does not mean being okay with who we have trained to be according to reification—a way that causes anxiety, despair, anger and harm to oneself and others— but being okay with ourselves as we truly are.

Even though we have been trained in a certain way through reification, we can choose another path. We do so when we begin to practice who we actually are through short moments. When we're introduced to short moments of awareness we can say,

"Aha! Of course, I knew this," and then with further practice it's easy to remember and to keep coming back to this recognition.

The teachings state that we are to let everything be *as it is*, and as a result of increasing familiarity with the teachings, we are in fact able to do so spontaneously. When we rest as our own reality and see everything *as it is*, we're happy and free and filled with energy. Once that change occurs for us, it's very convincing.

⊛∞⊛

The purpose of the teachings is to discover the genuine self. The genuine self, unlike the inauthentic self we have been trained in, is entirely spontaneous and cannot be held back. A genuine person spontaneously acts in accordance with who they actually are, rather than as who they are not.

We rest in the reality of ourselves, and this is how we know what is real. When we rest, we shift the perspective from confusion and doubt to assurance in our genuine, authentic self. The more we practice, the more authentic and genuine we become. As we become more authentic and genuine, we can be completely present with people and really see them. We can see that everyone shines with an inner light, even if their face is all gray and their countenance looks impenetrable and downcast. We don't have to try to do anything, like trying to see things in a particularly optimistic way.

There's the practice of what is real, and all virtue is already contained in what is real. Gradually we become more and more virtuous, but not virtuous according to the laws of society. We become virtuous according to the truth of our genuine self. More and more we can invite our genuine self—the nature of reality—to reveal itself.

Maybe some of you sit in meditation. I hope so, because I find that sitting meditation can be a wonderful adjunct to practice. It doesn't mean everyone has to do it. We always are who we are, and we respond to life according to our patterns. Whether it is with sitting meditation or without it, practice simply keeps pointing out over and over again our own inherent luminosity. Each short moment of practice is a short moment of accomplishment that reveals to us the nature of everything *as it is*, not as an intellectual concept, but as directly and properly perceived.

The authentic self isn't a new appearance; it doesn't come from another domain. When we recognize the genuine self, we are able to do things we were unable to do before, and it could be something that we never planned to do. Suddenly things come into their proper place, and there is an enormous leap in understanding one's purpose and one's direction in life.

An advanced practitioner who has had this enormous leap can sometimes be recognized by others, because that person is completely alert and responsive to other individuals. They're totally present as their genuine, authentic self. Some people can notice that something is different about such a person. What is different is the empathy and compassion that the person is radiating.

We become more alert through short moments, and life takes on a sharper-edged quality. A sign of accomplishment is that we are no longer living a blurry and confused life. Another sign of accomplishment is that we are full of an energy that gives us the endurance and the ability to fully engage with life—all of our life, until we die.

Please remember that when the word "accomplishment" is being used, it does not imply accomplishment in the usual sense of the word, as in efforting towards something and getting the expected result. Accomplishment in the way that it is meant here points to the natural unfolding of what is already present and available. So, a sign of accomplishment would be a capacity which is revealed through growing familiarity with open intelligence.

Dzogchen has incredible examples of endurance based on accomplishment. One of the examples is Wangdor Rimpoche, who carried Thuksey Rinpoche on his back all the way from Tibet to India. Endurance and energy are always-on, and the energy I am speaking about is the energy of life itself.

Our living energy has always been available to us, but its presence has usually not been so obvious to us. How unbelievable and incredible it is that Wangdor Rimpoche could have done what he did, and surely this is an inspiring example of the energy and endurance that are available to a human being.

Even if we feel like nothing is happening in our practice, it is happening. It is really happening, and sometimes other people can notice it. In my own case, I've had people who know nothing about Dzogchen say things to me that are a confirmation of my practice.

Giving one example, one person said, "I've never seen anyone show their genuine self like this before." I really appreciated that, because I was really being outrageous at the time, and the person is very traditional, so I didn't think I was going to have that kind of response, but I did. People often can recognize when we're being authentic.

❀

In whatever we see, awareness is present. The light that provides for the coloration of everything is always present, and our experience of this fundamental light comes through the incredible coloration that gives shape to everything. Within the colors is the light of everything. We have sound, and we have light and color, and as infants, sound, light and color were our primary "language," long before we began to use words.

However, for most of us, we don't feel like we have an understanding of our bodily or mental energies. To not have basic material goods is of course a very difficult situation to be in, but to not have a conscious connection with our own fundamental energy is a deficiency that generally goes unrecognized.

When we connect with the energy, we have a better sense that the qualities and activities of this energy are our own. If we feel that we have no awareness of this energy, then we can sit quietly and feel the warmth in our body. How magnificent this simple experience is. As long as there is life in the body, there is this warmth. The simple thought experiment of becoming consciously aware of the warmth that fills and sustains our body can lead us to be open to all the magnificent qualities and activities that are always present, but possibly hidden from us.

In the process of letting everything be *as it is*, we begin to live fully as we are without any reticence whatsoever, and perhaps also with a change in outward personality. For example, my own personality has changed over time. The authentic part of me was always there, but I had forgotten it or had not been able to locate it. For myself, I gradually became more directly empowered to live as I truly am, and as a result, my outward personality began to be expressed more in accordance with that.

In becoming more aware of our natural energy, the energy becomes the avenue for the expression of wisdom and skillful means according to our unique pattern. Individual, but not-individual; personal, but impersonal; apparently separate, but never separate....not and not-not. We are not a separate entity; we are an expression of an open intelligence of dynamic, sublime energy. Would this intelligence be everywhere else, but not in us as well?

Instead of thinking we're this separate person with all these personal attributes, we come to see ourselves in a much broader and universalized context. We come into a space of tremendous humility that brings us to a correct understanding of the way things truly are. This is really a cause of great celebration!

River water flows into the ocean, and in doing so the river water takes on the nature of the water of the whole ocean. There is no more river water; it is now water that has joined in the expanse and power of the entire ocean. When we rest, everything we see becomes the play of light, including ourselves. The merging with the light is similar to this analogy of the river and the ocean.

There are the eddies and waves in the vast ocean that are inseparable from the ocean, and in the same way, we are the play of the light that fills everything.

Our mind is clear and open and the points of light are the light of a great light within us. Essentially, that great light is what we are. We are the light from which the points of light are born.

WE KNOW THAT WE DON'T KNOW!

CHAPTER FOURTEEN

We have no idea what the future will bring, but for me as a practitioner, this lack of certainty is accompanied by an incredible sense of wonder and awe at the miraculous, magical nature of things. Part of this wonder is the gift of not-knowing. Not-knowing. In each moment, I don't know!

Humility is a key aspect of this practice, and when we come to the point that we know that we don't know, that is a sign of a flourishing practice. We know that we don't know. Of course, we have rational knowledge of things, and in that way we can know facts; however, what is being spoken about here is a broader definition of "knowing," in which there isn't a reliance on a reservoir of accumulated facts, assumptions and definitions.

When we admit that we don't know, we know a lot more about what we don't know. At one time in my life I couldn't possibly admit that I didn't know, but now it is fully clear to me that I don't know. How much better it is this way than having to know everything already. Knowing everything already all the time is such an energy drain.

"Not-knowing" is a matter of no longer being a collector of reified knowledge and solely relying on that accumulated knowledge. Instead of relying on acquired knowledge, we do whatever we do spontaneously and without an agenda in mind, and this spontaneous and skilled response does not come from an amassing of knowledge. We open up to aspects of ourselves that we have been denying ourselves without even knowing that we have done so. We come to see that we have incredible power within us to enact inconceivable activities.

❧

In my distant past I sometimes railed angrily at people, and I didn't know how to handle my feelings about them. However, thank goodness, I would eventually come to see that my responses were inadequate to the situation. I learned the hard way that the results could be better with another approach. It is so obvious that responses that come from rest are vastly different from those that come from reactivity.

We're human, so we go through life and we have concerns and challenges and pitfalls. When those concerns and challenges come up, the first thing we want to do is to rest and to practice. We practice out of the problem and into the solution. Practicing that way really results in the best solution.

If it's difficult for you to practice short moments, or even if you neglect the practice, please know that this can happen for anyone, and it's not an aberration. We may fall down, but we get up. We fall down again, we notice that we have fallen, and we get up again. The point is that we keep practicing, "Keep practicing"—that is the teaching.

All of us have lives that are sometimes smooth and other times filled with upset, and we can be assured of this. The good news is that upset and no-upset are each great arenas for practice. Rather than expecting constant smooth-sailing, we know that upset will occur, and we can practice for it and in it. We practice by resting as whatever appears.

We know that whatever appears has spontaneously appeared, and it will eventually spontaneously release. We really don't have anything to do other than practice. It is practice that will bring us to wisdom-insight and exaltation. A way to ensure this insight and exaltation is to address directly and skillfully what is coming up when it comes up.

Part of ongoing practice is to know that things like insight and exaltation are present and available. We gain confidence in ourselves, to the point of having complete confidence. In my younger life, I certainly didn't have complete confidence. I might have been bold at times, but temporary boldness is different from confidence. Confidence seeps in as we practice. We have more and more understanding, and we have more and more instinctive recognition of what the blessings of the teachings are.

By "blessings" I actually mean enrichment. The enrichment of the practice is forever enhancing our lives. As we continue to practice, we can feel the benefits that come with continued practice. When we get into a place where we're not feeling the benefits, we need to acknowledge this to ourselves and return to what has so lovingly nurtured us.

The devotion to clarity that is an integral part of the practice that I am describing here is required for us as a species. We need new solutions, and these solutions come from a luminous mind. Despite what we have been educated to believe, this luminous mind is always and forever our own mind. From the very beginning we carried the power of luminous mind with us into life. In each of the short moments we are practicing, we are practicing luminosity. This luminosity provides the rich resource of knowing that is the basis of not-knowing.

❧

All beings suffer, and the more I reflect on this fact, the deeper is my understanding and trust that suffering can also end. With reflection, my ability to connect with my own suffering and feel unbearable compassion for myself is greater. This compassion for oneself is the root of unbearable compassion for all. It isn't "unbearable" in that it is so overwhelming that we need to avoid it. Rather, it is the deeply heartfelt compassion and loving kindness that embraces all beings, and in this way it is a rich opportunity to further one's practice. I have approached this opportunity with fervor, as many others have as well.

When we rest as whatever is appearing, we're resting as its accommodation and potential, and we rest for short moments many times. In these teachings we've been empowered to practice short moments, and it is an unparalleled gift. In the future, there will be new methods for realizing who we truly are, and they will facilitate a different way of being human. They aren't even "methods" in the usual sense, and they don't require effort. It will be sublime activity that could be anything at all.

We have no idea what the future will bring, but for me as a practitioner, this lack of certainty is accompanied by an incredible sense of wonder and awe at the miraculous, magical nature of things. Part of this wonder is the gift of not-knowing. Not-knowing. In each moment, I don't know!

If we are feeling anxious about the future in this very changeable world, we can leave that strong feeling exactly *as it is*, with no need to change it or do anything to lessen even an iota of anxiety. Our anxieties are there simply because we have not known how to fully connect with ourselves, that's all. Fears and anxieties are not caused primarily by things or people, but by our perception of them. It always comes back to us and how we are choosing to perceive things.

❁

It is clear that we need a new language to describe what till now has generally not been described in a way that is understandable to a modern person, and a new global language of unity needs to come about. Today the teachings are being presented in a language that is comprehensible to many. More and more people know English and can read texts written in that language or in translation in their own native language. This fact, coupled with the modernization and optimization of the language of Dzogchen, has never occurred before. In this way, we have been born into an era of the greatest blessing.

We come to understand that the metaphors and the poetics of the texts of the teachings are waking us up from the slumber brought on by binary thinking. When we read or hear the texts, we know we're hearing something that is not like anything that we've heard before, and this can have a profound effect on us.

Humans don't live now the way we have lived in the past. There has been a great deal of innovation, discovery and invention over the past decades. We are a global culture now, and this global culture enacts itself differently than human culture has in the past. Why? Because there is more freedom. Even amidst many confining circumstances all around the world, humans have never been freer than they are today.

Why are these things important? For us as world citizens, we want to know about our fellow humans, and by understanding the ways in which people live together and the ways in which those conditions are changing, we can meet other beings in a full-hearted way. Today I feel it is a time when the teachings can be incredibly standardized in a modern form and language, but also customized so that there are unique approaches for each individual. When I consider the world, and when I reflect on human life, I want to take my practice and devotion all the way in order to alleviate the suffering in the world. I want to go to any lengths.

PEACEFUL MIND

CHAPTER FIFTEEN

Maybe through practice we will have a happy mind. Well, yes, we will; however, we'll have a fierce mind too, an enriching mind, a magnetizing mind and a peaceful mind. It's no longer a mind that is shaped into a limited form.

This resting practice can bring about a lot of power. We are able to do things that we previously thought were not possible, and we're able to do things without even feeling that we are doing anything. All of this is so new and so rich and thrilling, because we are being ourselves, and there's nothing better than that. Wherever we are, there we are.

When we utilize the teachings in a way that really confirms their value and worth, we're able to see things in a new way, and not only that, we're able to do things in a new way. This all comes from recognizing the genuine self. We might have been hesitant to face our fears and disappointments directly, but in practice we become more and more empowered. Practice brings about fearless confidence. That's one of the signs of accomplishment: fearless confidence.

It could be that we have truckloads of shame, and we may feel that we don't deserve to become who we truly are. But how could that be, when we already are who we are? The usual binary system of rewards and punishment, good and bad, shameful and exalted are opposites that only describe the false self and not the true self. We now have the opportunity to open up to the true self.

❧

Aggression is a pattern of society and we may have experienced a lot of aggression in our lives—towards others and also towards ourselves. To be aggressive and self-assertive is what people generally learn, and there is the subtle belief that aggressive behavior can produce a good result. Where and when has aggression, blame, hurt or harm allowed us to have genuine relationships with ourselves and other human beings? We know the answer to that, and I find the whole circumstance of aggression in the world very disquieting and unsettling.

The way to get a handle on this explosive aggressive energy is to make it workable through practice. Otherwise, it will continue to be an explosive energy that is difficult to contain. Practice transforms the energies that had previously driven us into reckless behavior. If we see that the aggression in us is diminishing in intensity, this is one of the signs that we are realizing the genuine self. The genuine self is the site of wisdom bliss—the great bliss and great love of wisdom.

When we feel aggressive, it is because we're working, working, working to keep a false sense of self in place. It is a self that has been fabricated, like in a factory of reification. But we no longer have to label ourselves something we're not. No matter who we are, no matter what our previous life has been, we are being invited to return to the authentic self in order to understand, recognize and realize the power that comes from pure perception.

In every short moment we are feeding our life with workability. We're no longer responding from reification, binary thinking and illusions; we are responding with clarity brought about by practice. When we practice, what is needed for us to flourish shows up. The evidence of practice is absolutely clear, and the evidence of no practice is also absolutely clear.

Maybe through practice we will have a happy mind. Well, yes, we will; however, we'll have a fierce mind too, an enriching mind, a magnetizing mind and a peaceful mind. It's no longer a mind that is shaped into a limited form. This peaceful mind is our touchstone with reality.

When we're new to the practice, there may be a lot of seemingly good reasons to be taken away from practice. But through short moments we build the habit of practice right into our day, all day long, no matter where we are or what we're doing. If doubt comes up and takes over everything else, that is a good time in which to engage with short moments—rather than taking ourselves away from the practice.

In doing so, we enter into the meditative flow and are much less troubled by what appears. The practice of short moments enlivens sublime body, speech, mind, qualities and activities, and in this enlivening we are being introduced to a more comprehensive intelligence.

To be comfortable in our own skin when we are feeling scared, doubtful and uncertain, we need to be gentle with ourselves. When in intense turmoil, we need to comfort ourselves like we would comfort a small child with kindness and care and understanding. Maybe when we feel we're not "getting it right" we feel forlorn, depressed, anxious, confused and so forth. If so, we rest, we let things be as they are, we develop our confidence in the practice and we allow a new understanding to emerge.

Instead of having a face in the mirror that is contorted and in pain, we can look at our image and there looking back at us is a warm, loving, contented face. This is our natural face, the face that reflects the way we actually are. The scenario I am describing here may sound silly, I don't know, but this is the face that we want looking back at us. This is the way our face is supposed to look.

The life we want to be leading is the one where it is this contented face that is in the mirror and not the other. The genuine self is expressive of what we really are, and through practice we allow the genuine self to emerge. This is the self that had been hidden from us by reification, but no longer.

The reified body and mind have been trained over time, so for a while we may continue to have the same responses as before, because we have been accustomed to responding in that way based on reified thinking. Like a potter's wheel that has been spinning but gradually comes to a halt, in the same way these negative responses will gradually diminish.

When we don't practice and we remain mastered by the reified responses, well, it will be a tough life, and I would not ever want to return there. We can't continue on encouraging all kinds of reified ideas and living from those ideas. No matter how long it has been that we weren't practicing, we can start practicing again at any moment. We can even begin practicing again in the midst of a complete breakdown. If we have stopped our practice for some reason, when else would we begin again but right now?

❁

In my earlier life I was often prone to very afflictive emotions. These were huge emotions that just welled up and took me over, and I felt that I could not do anything about them. The wish to come to terms with these emotions was one of my primary instigations and motivations to practice. Through my commitment to practice, I was able to come to terms with these emotions. I took all that afflictive energy and poured it into short moments.

Ah yes, short moments. Our awareness is directed away from sustaining the false separate self, and we're no longer trying to be anybody in particular. We're not trying to inhabit a role and act according to its definitions. In the reified world, this role-playing is what we're encouraged to do, but we don't need to follow this any longer.

We are blessed with an amazing intelligence that allows us the capacity to see the way things truly are, and we don't have to investigate this very much to validate that fact. We can look at the life of His Holiness the Dalai Lama, or we can look at Wangdor Rimpoche, who carried his teacher on his back from Tibet to India. In these lives we have a direct demonstration of what is being described here.

I am brought to tears by the kind of life I have and the great fortune I have found in Dzogchen. How is it possible that I have this blessing in my life, one that is very, very rare? How could this even happen to an American woman with no prior contact at all with Dzogchen? Well, we live in a time when there are great teachings being given. We live in a time of great masters who are available like never before. This is a most fortunate life to be born into, so why would I want to squander it?

❈

In some ways, devotion has been my only practice. Everything for me is centered in devotion. I give myself to the Dzogchen lineage and I am willing to go to any lengths to do what the lineage has asked of me. Through the blessings of the lineage, my entire focus is the benefit of all and the end of suffering—the enlightenment of all beings immediately—and that is what my activities are involved with.

The teachings that the Dzogchen lineage has so lovingly conveyed to us do not have to look any particular way. It is a matter of presenting the teachings in a way that is specific to this time of global community. We have the support from our gurus and the lineage to reveal what is ultimately true about ourselves.

Devotion became so much more clarified and elevated when I came to know my guru Wangdor Rimpoche, and doubly so when I came to know that he had carried his teacher from Tibet to India. When there are challenging things that come up for me, I reflect on Rimpoche carrying his guru this great distance in overwhelming circumstances. I reflect on Rimpoche saying over and over again that this was his greatest accomplishment in life. My relationship with Wangdor Rimpoche is such a generous gift to me, and every short moment in remembrance of him is a further gift.

We are naturally generous, and when we practice, that generosity becomes evident. Of course, we practice for ourselves and our own edification and illumination, but we also practice for the benefit of all. We practice for the basic sanity of all, for the good cheer of all, for the enlightenment of all.

There is so much unbelievable magic in life. This magic is "unbelievable" only because the mind of reason cannot believe it. But when we rest our mind, we know our genuine self—our genuine mind. With that we experience the magic and can walk out into the world and share the magic with others.

THE WISDOM OF DISCERNMENT
CHAPTER SIXTEEN

We don't go anywhere to realize anything; we realize it in ourselves as we are right now. That's always the case and is never otherwise. We have the tools in our life to do exactly what we want to do. Understanding what we really want to do is part of realization.

When we rest profoundly, the wisdom of discernment is revealed. But even before that, we might have had a greater understanding about how to speak and act, and this comes about naturally through rest. Every moment of practice is an initiation into wisdom and a refinement of wisdom, like refining gold. So, this is the intention: in every short moment of practice we discover and refine the gold.

The wisdom of discernment means that in each moment we act compassionately, and we can discern the entire situation we are dealing with and respond to it in a loving way. Our response might not look "loving" in terms of conventional ideas about loving. One might think that compassion is being nice all the time or never acting in any other way than what is considered to be "holy," but that need not always be the case.

Compassion could be expressed in any way, and it isn't necessarily going to look in every way like we might have imagined. My own experience is that sometimes purposefulness and skillful means come in forms that aren't necessarily warm and fuzzy. But it is clear, decisive, direct and totally dedicated to benefit.

Compassion is vast spaciousness and great, great depth. This spaciousness and depth is the way our mind actually is, not only for us, but also for everyone and everything. It could be a flower, a blade of grass, a subatomic particle or whatever else it may be, it is spacious and depthful and complete. It shines with the light of what is.

❀

We don't go anywhere to realize anything; we realize it in ourselves as we are right now. That's always the case and is never otherwise. We have the tools in our life to do exactly what is required of us. Understanding what we really want to do is part of realization. We come to see how we have been scripted in a life of reification to do particular things, but we find that we don't have to buy into what has been scripted for us.

We have powerful agency and autonomy innately within ourselves. We are such powerful beings, and we can open our intelligence to another level, where the focus is on service to all, rather than on our concern for ourselves and our own wants and needs.

Think about all the unpleasant things we go through in life— disappointments, defeats, betrayals and so forth. Human life is filled with this, but when we relate to these things through the power of the short moments practice and not through reified thoughts and emotions, we begin to feel grounded in our natural condition.

In life there's the possibility of experiencing travesty after travesty. Please know this. If there is no travesty now, there could be one later. What is more, sometimes in practice there can be a time when everything that we have taken to be true falls apart. I don't mean that it's necessarily a horrible experience. What has come up needs to be faced, and there's no way not to deal with it.

We cannot avoid tragedy or travesty in a human life, so we practice. There is nothing like very rigorous and extremely demanding situations to bring us to quick realization, because in those very rigorous situations, by resting deeply we find a path beyond struggle. So, for that reason, to be blessed with these teachings is such a gift, because we know where to turn when the going gets rough. To be resting doesn't mean that really tragic or even deadly things don't happen; it means that in the face of the tragic and deadly occurrence, we know what the vantage is that will carry us through.

No matter what is going on, we can choose to rest deeply and to not move away from that rest. With all of what occurs in life, resistance and anger can arise. Usually before we become angry, we feel increasing irritation or annoyance. If we rest deeply when we feel irritation and annoyance, that rest prevents us from going into anger or rage.

In terms of our speech and writing and what we post online or what we express in emails, it's important to communicate our realization, rather than an anger that is based on a limited idea of self. No matter what is going on in life, there really is no reason for us as practitioners to fall back into false and limiting ideas of the self and to express ourselves from that standpoint.

We can understand binary thinking, and we can enter into it if needed and know that it isn't going to harm us, and we can participate with a clear view of what's going on. We also can know that people saying bad things about us won't harm us. To remain clear and open and to not get caught up in abusive conversations can be a great demonstration of the practice.

We can show up for another way of life. We are not going to be dropping bombs on anyone, including anger bombs. If we practice anger and we allow annoyance and irritation to continue finding a secure home in us, it is like when a single drop of a chemical completely darkens an otherwise clear liquid.

If we think of someone and we say, "They were so nice and good before, but now they're really stupid and horrible," implicit in that is an intent to direct anger towards that person. It is a kind of angered disappointment with the person, one could say. But if we see everyone as they are through seeing ourselves as we are, we might still be at some level disappointed by the person, but we stay centered in our clear view despite the disappointment.

☸

If we are hoping for, praying for and wanting something really good for folks, we don't so easily become annoyed with them. We clarify who we are, and to do so is an incredible act, if for no other reason than that this clarifies and harmonizes our relationships with others. This clarity brings about gratitude for life itself and for everything and everyone in it, no matter what they're up to or how they represent themselves.

When we live life according to ordinary conventional understanding, we have little idea about what is truly possible. However, when we are practicing profoundly and freely, the wealth of practice comes into being. It could be that our life changes from what we had thought we were supposed to be and do.

Often that is the case, and our life becomes quite different from what we had previously expected. For example, I never expected to be in this role as a teacher. That was not in my mind at all. However, along the way I became clear on what my purpose is, and every day I become clearer still.

❀

As we clarify ourselves, we understand much more about who we are and what we're really meant to do in the world. Maybe when we came to the teachings, we were involved in one kind of activity. Then we began to practice, and after a while what we were involved in before doesn't feel as attractive as it had been.

Maybe we are hesitant to change our life circumstances because we have a career or we are committed to a certain situation. However, even if our situation or career doesn't change, we change, and then possibly along the way the situation can also change. But the situation can't change if we are overly invested in our thoughts, emotions and beliefs about the situation. This doesn't mean though that we can't have thoughts or emotions. The emotions are wisdom in their essence, so we simply need to understand what the emotions actually are.

We might come across something that we had rejected in the past. An example in my life was how I had once rejected Tibetan Buddhism. I thought that it was superstitious and a way to take away people's power to act, but those were my very uninformed views. I had already been practicing for a long time, but I still was unclear about some things.

It is sometimes possible to reject something as worthless because of previously held beliefs. I didn't act in that extreme way, but I did feel, "I don't want to do that particular practice, and I wouldn't suggest it to anyone else." But once I met the great gurus from Tibet who became my teachers, I radically changed my point of view.

The knowledge that everything is complete in itself comes about through resting. We begin to understand that everyone, no matter who they are and no matter what they're doing, can be seen as a teaching for us. This is the way we practice, and this is one aspect of our skillful means to benefit others.

If we feel confused and that the confusion is impeding our progress, we rest in the confusion and seek support if possible. With deep reflection and compassion, we begin to dissolve the confusion, but not by beating it to death or trying to change the shape of the confusion. We dissolve the confusion by resting utterly and completely as we are. To be able to rest as these very potent energies arise is the source of great wisdom and empowerment.

This practice is about being so kind to ourselves that we begin to understand that we really have no essential defilements. To think that we have essential and inescapable defilements is simply something we've learned about ourselves, but it is untrue. We are not defiled and we cannot be, because we always are who we are.

Section Three:

A GROWING FAMILIARITY

17. The Road Less Traveled By   110

18. Ultimate Comfort   116

19. Vulnerability   122

20. A Comprehensive Intelligence   128

21. What Connects Everyone   134

22. Inconceivable   140

23. Self-Educating   146

24. A Sense of Delight   152

THE ROAD LESS TRAVELED BY
CHAPTER SEVENTEEN

You may know the poem from Robert Frost, "The Road Not Taken." In the poem, the narrator came to a fork in the road and, "Took the one less traveled by, and that has made all the difference." As practitioners, we have chosen the road less traveled by, because we could see that the traveled road would not satisfy us.

What we have named and described through binary thinking is an illusion, and an illusion cannot support us in difficult times when support is desperately needed. No matter what conventional notions we have relied on, they will never be fully sufficient, and because they are never fully sufficient, we suffer. When we practice, we begin to see through the illusion, and this recognition gives us even greater motivation to practice.

Everything is impermanent; everything is in flux. We never see the same thing twice, because it is constantly changing. If we close our eyes briefly and then open them again, change has occurred. The thoughts come one at a time and then pass away. They don't come in huge groups; they come one at a time, and there is only a perceived connection between them. When we say something is "this" or something is "that," there really isn't a connection between all the words in that sentence.

There are two primary delusions, first, that we are somebody, and second, that we're doing something. That statement might sound unfamiliar at first, but the more we become confident in our short moments practice, the less unfamiliar it becomes, and the more we see that we no longer have to live inside the cocoon of conventional notions. When we know the nature of reified perception to be illusory, without even thinking about it or trying to do anything, we become much more alert—and radically compassionate.

When we practice diligently and with perseverance, insights begin to come to us. For instance, regardless of how we have seen the world from a cause-and-effect, rationalistic vantage, we now begin to see how we have been caught up in illusions. What an astounding statement to consider!

❦

Practicing positive affirmations is a great illusion as well; however, positive affirmations and practicing positivity are very popular in today's world. Maintaining positive states in order to be upbeat is especially popular now, especially in youth culture, and it is believed that positivity is something that will uphold a person. Maybe it will be somewhat supportive when they're young, but as people age, they suffer more and more bodily humiliations, and such a practice of positivity cannot be successfully sustained.

I encourage everyone to not fall prey to this urge to rely on positive affirmations, because practicing positivity neutralizes all the negativity we're repressing, but in fact, the negativity is where the greatest wisdom is. So, why would we want to repress it?

We have learned to give the energy in our body an independent nature, so we have named it things like "anger," "despair" or "fear," but rather than combating these emotions through positivity, we rest as the energy without naming it. Overwhelming fear, fear like we've never had before, might seize us, but we don't run away. We rest in the energy of that fear. We are not taken over by fear when fear arises.

No matter what the negativity is we may be dealing with, we don't want to cover it over with positivity. We want to rest with the negative energy, rather than trying to push it away. Everything is simply *as it is*, and there is impartiality about what appears in each moment. That is what one sees and responds to:

what is right here, in this moment, without the burden of naming it.

Wisdom—unlike practicing positivity—is not erratic. It is an always-on, primordial intelligence that is expressed in wisdom-exaltation and sublime activities.

You may know the poem from Robert Frost, *The Road Not Taken*. In the poem, the narrator came to a fork in the road and, "Took the one less traveled by, and that has made all the difference." As practitioners, we have chosen the road less traveled by, because we could see that the traveled road would not satisfy us. We have been introduced to something that will support us to be freer and more complete. It is a way of being that is an expression of primordial wisdom, one which is entirely different from the way we've been while moving along the more traveled road.

We practice to the point where we no longer are avoiding negativity, and in order to practice to accomplishment, it requires being willing to feel really miserable, depressed, awful—worse than we've ever felt in our life—because we are no longer pushing things down or avoiding the negativity. Instead, we can allow everything to be *as it is*.

We all have things that we have repressed or suppressed, and to fully rest with those things is extremely powerful. We are no longer so easily overwhelmed as we were before, so that's good news, too. When it feels like we have more than we can handle, we can rest and also connect deeply with other beings, because support is so helpful in tough times.

Sometimes we may be really afraid of the emotions that come up, but it is essential to not push them away. We can now welcome all the meanderings of the mind that we may have rejected in the past, even the thoughts and emotions that have hurt so much. This lack of rejection leads to the sort of opening that reveals so much that had been hidden. No longer do we need to rely on artifice, pretense or avoidance to protect ourselves.

No matter who we are, when we face an unexpected situation in everyday life, things can be challenging. When we have unexpected events that we describe as bad or wrong or something we did not want or plan on, often it's so upsetting that we have no idea what to do. However, happily, we have the capacity within us to see the way forward. It may seem like we don't have the capacity, only because in our culture we have not been encouraged to rest with and accommodate the afflictive emotions.

❦

At some point we will realize that all of this energy is within us, that the wisdom is within us, and that we've never really been practicing with something outside ourselves. Realization is not something somewhere else that we can go to the store and buy. As we gain more confidence, we know that we can rest in the energy of whatever arises. We have trained ourselves to have all kinds of different energy: "Oh, this is anger, fear and depression." However, when we rest in it and as it, we are able to see these things in a much different light.

Great joy is one of the accomplishments of the practice. It is great bliss, and in this bliss—the sun kissing the moon—we feel complete. All of it is worth it: the pain is worth it, and the ecstasy is worth it too. When we practice, our joys become even greater joys. They become joys that envelop everything. At first, it's our ordinary human joy, but in the end it is the discovery of bliss, sublimity and exaltation. This is who we are, naturally so.

When we get sick and we can't do anything about the illness, there are all kinds of emotions that come up. What can we do? We rest as those emotions as well. When we can meet severe illness in this way, we can then meet death in the same way, and we no longer have the same fear we had before. Any of us could die at any moment, and typically there is a lot of fear surrounding the thought of death. People are afraid of death only because they have not been properly prepared for it.

What is more, possibly within each human being is the secret irrational notion that, "I can't imagine actually dying, so maybe I will somehow be immortal." But you see, we *already are* immortal, so we don't have to try to get there! We practice in preparation for the death of the physical body, and not in some futile hope that the body will go on forever. In practice, we come to know ourselves as we truly are, and we see that our immortality is already right here.

These teachings were originally developed as a death practice, and the practices we are speaking about here permit us to die well. I have had many questions along the way, and for me there has definitely been this curiosity about the nature of death. I feel so fortunate that I have these glorious teachings to guide me into death.

❈

So much of what we have been taught is concerned with acquiring things, like say for instance, buying a house, getting what we want and having a lot of possessions. Why is that desire there? An aspect of that desire is that we want to conform to the norm. We want to fit in with what everyone else is doing.

We don't generally think very deeply about this willingness to conform, and it is likely that many will not investigate this in their lifetimes. But with practice we do think about these important things. We can inquire, "How am I living my life in response to these acquired desires?" Whatever is going on for us, we can rest as the open intelligence that is ever our own. It's our gold; it's the true wealth that cannot disappear.

The more we practice, the more riches we receive that are not transitory. We may accumulate lots of money, buy all of what we think will bring us happiness, eat good food, drink fine wine, wear nice clothes and live in a spacious house; however, none of this is going to make us completely happy, and it will all eventually pass away.

What about when we get old and our body starts to fall apart? We become very ill, and we finally have a condition that we won't recover from. The illness gets worse and worse, and then we die. Will the money and clothes and nice house go with us at death?

Even in very wealthy areas, people's lives can be surprisingly desperate. This can also be true for a person who has not only great wealth, but also name and fame and position in society. But without basis or foundation in wisdom—even with great wealth and fame—fundamental happiness can be elusive.

Accumulating money for the sake of wealth alone is a futile task. It's never going to make us completely and ongoingly happy. What would we have if we had all the money in the world? Would it protect us from the rages of nature? Would it save us at death? Absolutely not. We leave it all behind when we depart.

However, there is another vantage on this. If we as practitioners had the exact same kind of life I just described, where we were living in the wealthiest community and we were known by people all over the world, we wouldn't have the same experience as the people who are so desperate. Why? Because we would be practicing, and whether there were riches or no-riches, we would know where our true wealth lies.

ULTIMATE COMFORT

CHAPTER EIGHTEEN

Everything and everywhere is a place of practice. When we practice regardless of what is going on, we are showing up fully for life.

One could die at any moment, and this is true for all of us. That's what the teachings are about: that we can die at any moment. No matter what adversity comes up, through practice it can be used as a preparation for death. A good thing to ask is, "How will this present experience help me prepare for death?" Practicing in this way might sound sad or even morbid to some people, but I don't think it sounds that way to anyone who has reaped the benefits of this practice.

Practitioners can recognize the depths of suffering, how much each of us suffers, and that there is no one who is an exception to the suffering. Everything and everywhere is a place of practice. When we practice regardless of what is going on, we are showing up fully for life. If we don't like the situation we're in and if it's diminishing or not supportive, we can change it. Whether changing a situation or not, we can practice while doing either of them.

We simply show up as we are and practice, and through that we experience the reward of knowing what to do. If change needs to occur, we can skillfully bring it about. In many cases the "saying, doing and changing" won't conform to a lot of our prior ideas. We could say anything at all and we could do anything at all, but we come to that spontaneously and capably.

❧∞❧

Our expression in life becomes clear to us, but that doesn't mean that this clarity will be understandable to everyone else. We may very much want it to be clear to our family, colleagues, friends and society in general, but that doesn't mean that it will be. Some people might think we're great, others will think we're horrible, and like a friend told me once, "Most won't care."

Trying to cultivate someone so that they will like us is no longer a lifestyle choice. If we have the confidence gained by practice, we go where we need to go and do what we need to do without concern. Even if the fruits of practice won't be evident to many others, for those who are interested, through their openness they can actualy *see* the other person and thereby be introduced to this way of being.

Even when we are grounded in our true selves, it might look like we're engaging with data streams in an ordinary way. We're talking and acting and showing up and giving to the world in a manner that people might feel is familiar to them, but which in fact is not ordinary at all. There are stories in the Tibetan tradition of great beings called "mahasiddhas," who demonstrate so vividly that realization has a very wide reach and display. Realized practitioners do all kinds of things, say all kinds of things and have all kinds of expressions, but it all comes from deep realization. This realization is available not only to certain people, but to all human beings.

This is another reason to talk about the great mahasiddhas. They have all kinds of manifestations, like being a beggar, a prostitute, an apparently crazy person, on and on and on. This fact alone is a great message for us. The mahasiddhas are incredible beings who perform incredible feats, and that accomplishment does not need to look any certain way.

It's important to understand that any power anyone has, including the power of the great mahasiddhas, we potentially have it as well, and the more we practice, the more that this is evident. It doesn't mean that each of our expressions will be exactly the same, because we're each so unique in our personality and in the way that we show up.

We each have marvelous emanations that are shining from us all the time. More and more we realize that we are a marvelous emanation of everything. We can go anywhere; we can do anything. Yes, we are different and unique, and yet, when we look out at all the world, we see *ourselves*.

We certainly see many fearsome things today, and we can count on more of these fearsome things in our world. It seems like the suffering will never end. However, everyone has the choice to practice—or not—and a practitioner receives the benefits of the practice. No matter how unbearable or fearsome things might be, there's always the knowledge and wisdom available that will give ultimate comfort.

When we begin the practice, we may not have ever experienced a moment of total relief, but that's what the introduction is—the first moment of total relief. In that moment is everything that we are. Even though we might be practicing in relation to something that's really bugging us, it isn't about the bugging. It's about our understanding of what the bugging actually is in its essence.

Are we going to allow things to take us off course from our practice? When something comes up that pokes us, we can choose to practice. The more we do so, the more we have the result. We have the result not only when we're in a teaching setting or when we're sitting on a cushion, but we find that we have the result regardless of what the situation is.

Nothing is done to avoid the afflictive situation; the relief comes simply from our realization again and again of what is truly so. In that moment of realization, we hold dear the basic space that we all are, and when we do this over and over again, it's like building a muscle.

For each of us, what is really important is to realize that our core essence cannot be distorted by data-stream descriptions. When we feel disturbed in any way, we often feel the energy in our body associated with that disturbance. We've learned to call things "depression," for example, because we've heard over and over again that certain displays are "depression." However, what we believe to be depression is at its basis the energy of sublime wisdom and skillful means.

☘

If we're looking for love, where is the best place to find it? Some of us learned that we can find a heightened love in religion or in philosophy, one that isn't based in all the messy everyday stuff. Others of us try to find love through romantic relationships, but often that may subtly occur within the transactional context of, "I will love you if you love me."

Anxiety and fear are fundamental in a relationship that is based on transactional love. We're expecting love from the other person and we fear we won't get it, so there's an underlying anxiety. Maybe we looked for stability in a partnership or friendship of some kind. We want stability, so we want that love from the other person to be enduring.

This ability to generate loving relationships and connections, to really live in a space of perfect loving is, I feel, the essence of human life. Real love can't be calculated. So, say, in a romantic and intimate relationship, the relationship no longer needs to be transactional and isn't determined by what the other person does or doesn't do, gives or doesn't give. Instead, there is an atmosphere of love that is always present. This situation is so much more satisfying and easeful, because the other forms of transactional love require so much work.

When we practice very deeply, we can more clearly see the ways in which we've been led to try to get happiness and not have unhappiness. We see how we have been trying to get love, but never being able to fully find it, because relative love is impermanent. That's just the way it is: it's impermanent.

Love is not a transaction, and neither is it mere reciprocity or the coldness of duty. Love is radical and all-encompassing and the basis of all skillful means. When we find out that love isn't just a feeling, and we hear about a love that is not based solely on context, it is exciting, because now we're dealing with something long-lasting, rather than something that's coming and going.

More and more we realize that the love that we're realizing is naturally present. We trust that nothing is being done, there is no one doing it, and there is no final consequence to anything we do. How could there be a final consequence, when every single event is impermanent? How could we ever possibly have a definitive result to an action?

❈

There is this energy in our body that we've called by all sorts of names, but now we can understand it as our resting place. It is the place of all of our power and beneficial activity. When we take a short moment, we are resting as that energy itself, and this reveals a treasure trove of experience and of accomplishment.

The reified mind and its thoughts are always getting our attention, and it seems that the thinking mind is all that we are, but any kind of meaning that comes from thoughts is made up. We only have one thought at a time, and one thought is not connected to another one, even if it seems that they all connect together. Look at your thoughts and see that the thought now has nothing to do with the next thought, even though we might think that we have a rational string of thoughts going on.

We're taught to believe that we're identical to our psychological and physical states. The fact is that we rarely think, "I am someone," but when we do, it's best to practice and see that the idea that "I am someone" is impermanent. It comes and then it

120

goes. This self-identity is a feature of our reified mind, a data stream, but it doesn't mean that it's true. We've been told over and over again that we are "someone," and then we start to describe ourselves in that way.

This false way of being is demeaning to our magnificence and diminishes our ability to be exactly who we are. No one else can stop us from being who we are; we are the only ones who can stop ourselves. We need to sincerely and fervently take these teachings on, rather than just trying to figure out what they mean. We take them on for ourselves, practice them and enjoy all the magnificent benefits!

VULNERABILITY

CHAPTER NINETEEN

Vulnerability need not be a sometimes thing; it can be an all-the-time thing. We can recognize vulnerability as a friend that can support us in resting and which allows us to see things from a new vantage.

Great vulnerability is available in each short moment. Our inherent vulnerability is available, even when we're trying to do something else, like trying feverishly to defend ourselves or trying to contrive confidence and fearlessness. We haven't learned that our vulnerability itself is the source of fearlessness and confidence. It sounds like it would be the opposite, but it isn't, but that fact is too much for binary thinking to comprehend.

When I was growing up, my focus was on *in*-vulnerability. I was learning to be invulnerable, and I developed a fear of being vulnerable. When I began allowing myself to feel vulnerable and totally open—and finding that it was extremely helpful to do so—I realized what a rich resource we all have. This resource is the empowerment in knowing that there is nothing in the mind to hold on to and no mind to hold on to it. The reified mind looks for something to hold on to, but the notion that anything can be held on to is illusory. To try to hold on to something or defend something isn't going to lead anywhere.

Instead, we rest completely and allow even the most afflictive feelings to be as they are. In their vividness these feelings become a resource, just like a gold mine is a resource. Any of us in this moment can feel vulnerable and authentic. Vulnerability is not something that is distant and inaccessible, nor is it like a haunting figure that's going to jump out and frighten us.

As we become vulnerable enough to allow our authentic self to reveal itself, a great deal of intuition and insight becomes available to us. In vulnerability, we skillfully show up for whatever is coming our way, and we are authentic while doing so.

We might feel scared to death to share with others what has scared us to death. We might feel ashamed to say we feel ashamed, but candid disclosure about oneself is one of the aspects of being authentic and vulnerable. It isn't like when we are applying for a job and we have to prove our qualifications and hide our weaknesses. Being authentic means being who we actually are and not who we have been trained to be. There are no masks any longer.

⊕⊃⊂⊕

The greatest introduction to vulnerability comes in seeing that there is absolutely no thought or image to hold onto, and with a loving heart filled with vulnerability and courage, there's no longer the same desire to hold onto reified things. Any perception we have instantaneously self-releases, and it is the loving heart that is able to show up in the space of spontaneity with complete calm and openness to whatever is appearing. This is the way we really are: completely spontaneous, open and vulnerable.

Vulnerability need not be a sometimes thing; it can be an all-the-time thing. We can recognize vulnerability as a friend that can support us in resting and which allows us to see things from a new vantage. Yes, recognizing vulnerability as a friend, instead of racing to use the mind to create a false sense of safety and security.

I would like to invite everyone to feel vulnerable and raw. Think of something in your life that feels threatening, but instead of withdrawing into fear, feel the energy in your body that is vulnerable and raw.

When we think of ourselves as only being a body, all we have then is our skin and bones and organs. But what ultimate satisfaction are those going to give us? Our skin can be ripped off, all our bones broken, and death can come at any moment. By going through an inquiry like this, in which we investigate the true nature of our ephemeral body, we are allowing ourselves the opportunity to grow more familiar with vulnerability.

Sometimes when individuals allow themselves to feel totally vulnerable, they can also possibly feel alone. Yes, not only vulnerable, but also alone, and that they can't share what they are discovering with anyone else because the ideas would be unacceptable. This is what I have felt, because in my lifetime my ideas haven't been suitable to many people. But now I'm inspired by rawness and vulnerability!

I'm also inspired by softness and tenderness, and these come from being totally present in vulnerability. Instead of having it be a one-off like, "I'm vulnerable for now, but I don't know about the future," it is always-on openness. This is the space of realization. This is where we find wisdom-exaltation and sublime activity.

When we are completely available and vulnerable in relationship with others—and they are the same with us—we create a situation where we can flourish together. Not only do we grow and flourish together, but the benefits coming from such a relationship are spectacular. In our loving, entirely vulnerable relationship with one another, we do not know what will happen next. We can fully trust one another within a context of shared vulnerability.

That is another aspect of vulnerability: the willingness to not know what will come next. Each of us will face all kinds of unexpected occurrences in life, as we already have, and many of the events we will face will include things we won't like.

However, in all times, places and circumstances we can rest as ourselves.

There's no way to totally manage what will come next. Wow, look at the vulnerability in just acknowledging that! Even if we have some notion of what will come next, what does come next will not exactly match that notion. We can then humbly say what I say to myself, "I know nothing." I really do not know anything, because it's a waste of time to try to build ideas into something. We could be of the opinion that we know a lot, but I would much rather know that I don't know.

This is a teaching that states that everything is within us. One doesn't need to run around trying to change things on the outside. The relationship with things on the outside changes because of the adjustment that occurs inside. Let me repeat that because it is so important: the relationship with things on the outside changes because of the adjustment that occurs inside.

The gift of realization is that we can be in any circumstance, whether the circumstance is seen to be hideous or wonderful. By letting it be *as it is*, the circumstance is known to be equal and even. This is one of the many incredible ideas we come across when we practice. Some of these ideas may seem like they couldn't possibly be the case, when in fact they are.

✿

Almost all of us grow up with some, or a lot, of pain and hurt. We know that we have the pain and we want to do something about it. If through the teachings we now know what to do with our pain and hurt, then out of compassion we want to ensure that others can feel the same relief we have felt.

If I'm with people who could generally be seen as troublesome, I want to be able to be there with them gracefully. That's what I want: I want to be graceful. I'm not there to beat anybody into submission, and they are not something I need to run away from.

I want to listen, to see what's going on and to really be present with the person and be entirely open and vulnerable in the encounter. I want to be with the energy in a way that is completely unafraid.

I want to join with that energy, knowing that it is my own. The energies we have are indivisible from the union of all energies that are. The energies that are, are the luminosity of emptiness— its accommodation and potential in the world that we see and the worlds we don't see, the beings we see and the beings we don't see. Dzogchen states that emptiness is luminous; it is not a void. It is that luminous accommodation and potential of everything that is appearing.

There may be times in our lives when we have a complete breakdown. Things change dramatically, and suddenly we're left in a new state of affairs, one we probably didn't expect, and we have no idea what to do. Maybe none of you have ever felt like that, but I have felt that way repeatedly. But each calamitous incident in our lives is a treasure chest filled with vulnerability and potential.

I don't mean by this that I am trying to restore good feelings so that I can feel okay. I never, ever want to do that. Why? Because I'm a practitioner and I'm seriously dedicated to resting in the midst of all that arises. We all have all kinds of mental events, and I know that for some of you, many of your mental events may seem to you to be entirely lunatic-crazy. You know how I know that? By looking in the mirror at myself. I know what it's really like because I have been there myself. Vulnerability.

❁

When we totally feel our energies, we are feeling our being, and we are identifying with our actual self, our actual identity, our genuine self. This is why it feels so complete. It may feel a little scary at first, maybe off-and-on scary or all-the-time scary, but it will just be however it is. Instead of having energy pulled out to ideas that don't work for us, through resting as our own energy, we are guided. It's like a laser light guiding us exactly to where we need to go.

We need to show up with an all-encompassing perceptual toolkit in order to get a clear sense of what's happening. We may be dealing with something, and today it looks one way, while tomorrow it looks another way, and our actions could be different each day. But we remain open and vulnerable, and we are no longer trying to conform to a way of being that is defined by conventional beliefs.

At one time I thought of perception as something specific, as in, "I perceive this." However, the more I practice, the more I see that perception belongs to no one. The terms we perhaps have read about, like "all-seeing" or "all-knowing" for example, relate to what I have just said. We really are the all-seeing perceiver of everything and not an individual being.

For me, there's always this sense of expansion and inclusion and more expansion and inclusion, but without anything going on. It's a pure sense of energy. This has been called "presence" in many teachings. By relying on the energies of our body, we become present without trying to be present.

There is no reason that we all have to be alike, because each one of us has our own unique display and gifts to give. We are not a uniform expression that needs to be tailored to a certain size and shape. Instead of being shaped like we have been before by reified ideas that don't belong to us, we come back to our true selves and give integrity to our own experience, and we flourish. We flourish. What glorious teachings these are, teachings that have been so generously given to us so that we can flourish. I feel so very fortunate.

A COMPREHENSIVE INTELLIGENCE

CHAPTER TWENTY

What do we want for ourselves? Do we want happiness, confidence and sublime bravery? Is this what we want our energy to be used for, or do we want to continue to have our energy directed in all kinds of ways that lead to suffering? The best we can do in making this decision is to be totally clear, vulnerable and authentic.

The energy in our body is powerful. This can be known from the beginning of our practice, because when we have an authentic introduction, we are introduced to this powerful energy. This powerful energy is the sublime force that pervades everything.

The practice of short moments is an opening into realization, but because at first we cannot identify it as such, it seems like we need to be going somewhere else or accomplishing something to reach the realization. When we take a short moment, we are tapping into sublime bravery, a bravery and a confidence that is unlike anything else, because it doesn't come from self-focus, arrogance or competition. Rather, it comes from the wish to bring benefit to oneself and to others. Everything in life can be devoted to bringing benefit to oneself and others.

A more comprehensive intelligence has a totally different perspective when compared to binary thinking. A comprehensive intelligence doesn't rely on binary thinking, but can know when it might be needed. Even when binary thinking is employed, it is exalted, because the person employing that form of thinking is acting from a comprehensive intelligence.

❦❧

The teachings state that there is suffering, but in a way, I wish it were stated that there is *unbearable* suffering. There is unbearable suffering. Especially for Dzogchen practitioners, there is a strong sense of how much suffering there is and that the suffering is unbearable. But the compassionate Buddha made it clear that there is an end to suffering and that there are the tools available to end it.

Most of us have never learned that we have profound qualities and activities that are far beyond imagination. We're all born with a precious jewel in our hand. There isn't anyone who is not a buddha, even if, without proper training, the exalted concept of "being a buddha" can be misinterpreted. To say that we are in essence a buddha may seem daunting and even impossible for some who hear it.

In Dzogchen, the fact is emphasized that we suffer because we do not know that things are impermanent. Despite that, there is often the idea that people have of trying to put something permanent in place and to hold it there, like for example attaining a realization and then holding it in place.

That is an erroneous assumption, because there is no place where the realization is, other than right here, right now, already present and available—inside you, inside me, fully present in me, fully present in you. It is not something to be attained and then held onto. When this realization dawns in us, it gives us what we need to live a wonderfully beneficial life. We will find the confidence, the intelligence, the perfect love and also the humor and joy that are already our own.

Now with the network of communication around the world, we see that there is so much unbearable suffering in the global community of beings. In the past, people might have only been aware of the suffering for themselves and their families and their local community, but now through the power of the internet we have more familiarity with what people are experiencing all over the world. We are no longer only identified with our families or countries; we're now identified with a global community.

It had never been possible before for the entire world to be united in a common purpose, but now with the online world being more and more exposed to great teachings, it becomes possible for us to elevate each other. I don't see this elevation of one another as an unattainable goal; I see it as exactly what is wanted and needed.

In my younger years, what I had been told would give me a happy life didn't give me a happy life, and I didn't know what to do. I still had to figure it out for myself, as we all do. I had already practiced a form of short moments in my life, but once I had the giving energy and generosity of the Tibetan gurus poured all over me, I started to get busy with the fact that all of my intellectual posturing was really not going to get me anywhere, which is where it had already gotten me!

My gurus had the graciousness to do me the great service of introducing me to Dzogchen and giving me the guidance that is needed along the way. Every single time I was with my own guru, Wangdor Rimpoche, he had exactly the same sustained disposition. It never changed. He was very peaceful, and he was also magnetic and enriching. I see now how his magnetic presence was a form of instruction and how purposeful these intimate instructions were, because they claimed victory over the fear and doubt that had been present in me.

It was disconcerting for me in my earlier life that I had to try to make sense of the world through binary aspects, such as positive and negative or good and bad. With practice though, at some point I couldn't get on board with this binary view any longer, and I couldn't see things in any other way other than how I knew them to actually be.

At first this vantage did seem a little remote, but when I met Wangdor Rimpoche, I suddenly felt such a great devotion to him and to the teachings, and I knew that I was in the right place. I could feel the incredible love that brought the great gurus to be who they are—that incredible force of love that will never go away. My confidence in the teachings grew exponentially, and the allegiance to binary thinking fell away.

I knew there was an incredible force of perfect love that would never go away, and this is what I had been looking for. I yearned to meet someone who had realized this incredible force of perfect love, and when I met the great Tibetan gurus, including Wangdor Rimpoche, I was convinced: "This is the real deal," just like I might say if I found a physicist or mathematician who is exceptional and who could fully reveal math and physics to me. I feel that by having such a desire to know the truth, the truth comes into our life in a way that we can't set aside. It is *as it is*, and we know we're not getting away from it, ever.

My own gurus allowed me to see exactly how they live, with nothing left out. I got to see it all. However, not all gurus are the essence of peace like these that I have spoken about, and there are gurus who express the essence of peace in conduct that seems crazy.

Some are known for being especially wild and crazy. "Yeshe cholwa" is Tibetan for crazy wisdom. Why do the Tibetans have a term for crazy wisdom? Because they know how important devotion is, and they know that a devotional relationship can also involve "crazy" behavior on the part of a guru. Or better said, the way of being of these gurus can seem crazy to those who don't yet understand its instructive power.

Why is it "crazy"? Could it be called something else to make it clear what is involved? The way I think about it is that this apparently crazy behavior comes from a more comprehensive intelligence. For those who don't have a vantage of comprehensive intelligence, the instructive power of those who do have that comprehensive intelligence can seem bizarre and inappropriate.

What is for sure is that the expression of crazy wisdom does not involve thinking about things or contemplating a plan of action. It is an entirely spontaneous and unfettered expression of benefit. For some of us who are of the think-think-thinking variety, to be entirely spontaneous and free of conceptions would be a relief. There is in fact nothing conceptual to hang on to.

❦

What do we want for ourselves? Do we want happiness, confidence and sublime bravery? Is this what we want our energy to be used for, or do we want to continue to have our energy directed in all kinds of ways that lead to suffering? The best we can do in making this decision is to be totally clear, vulnerable and authentic.

Thoughts, emotions and feelings don't tell us anything true about ourselves. The boot camp of binary logic and reason brings us only misery. We may not realize that there is often a pervasive lurking fear operating for us, and out of that fear comes despair and distress.

If we look at the ways that we have used our minds, we might feel ashamed and embarrassed to let anyone else know about it. However, in a sangha (*community*) and in a teaching setting we can feel safe, because everybody is in the same place. We may not all have had the same twists and turns in our lives, but each of us can see how our particular and unique emotional states have been trained into us by our life circumstances.

We have been trained through binary thinking to believe that our energy is localized within us as thoughts, emotions and sensations and that we are totally independent beings. This is a big idea in the West: that we are independent entities and creators. This kind of talk makes me giggle now because it is so off-base.

The benefits of this wonderful practice are, well . . . I wouldn't know where to begin. I could start listing them and I don't know when I would end. I do know that my life is wonderful and that I am happy, confident and able to do things that at one time I would have considered completely inconceivable for me. None of these things were something that I could have imagined or planned for in my life. I think it has to be very rare to be a Dzogchen practitioner, and to have been granted these sorts of gifts is even rarer still.

When we come to the practice, we enter into delight. It feels so different, so new and so fresh, and it can take some time to adjust to this new way of being.

I'm here to serve. That's what I want to do, I want to be of benefit and I want to live in harmony with others. I feel that I have been given a golden life. Yes, this is truly a golden life. It is a precious gem. We have this precious wisdom-mind that fills us. Our entire body is the wisdom-mind and it has never been anything else.

WHAT CONNECTS EVERYONE
CHAPTER TWENTY-ONE

Here we are all together; we are all sharing a reality that we each experience as individuals and that we experience together. We are able to go down the street loving those we meet, loving them so thoroughly and totally and without any pretense, because we really know who we are and who they are.

It is good to remind ourselves as practitioners that all of us are celebrants of the same religion: a way of living that connects everyone. We're connected by what is so basic to all of us that it can never be denied. The point of our practice is the recognition of the magnificent energies that are in us which unite us with everyone—not given to us from someone else or by an All-Creator—but as the spontaneity of pure presence itself.

And yet, every single one of us is entirely unique. Even though we're always linked at a foundational level—the sublime essence of what is—our lives are a display of what looks like difference. Our patterns change according to our distinctive way of being. We are unique, yet we practice in a united way according to our uniqueness. If we had been placed in some other situation vastly different from the one we are in now, we would have another display and another pattern.

This idea of a separate identity that we have created is an illusion, which also includes the illusion of separate things: the ocean, the earth herself, the universe and whatever else is perceived. Once we recognize how things truly are, we begin to have the freedom to make the choices that unite us, rather than separating us out. How did we develop this self-identity that seems so fixed and separated out? It happened by being trained in reification.

❧☙

All of our life is simply an always-changing pattern of transformation of energy. We are nothing else other than that energy. In reified thinking, we seem to be in the position of needing to recover something we lost, but which in fact we have always already had.

When we first begin the resting practice and all of the energy in us becomes obvious, it might be a little frightening, or, it could be a great relief. Even if it is frightening, rest as it anyway, and it will become an expression of bodhicitta—for oneself, because we must first have self-compassion—and then bodhicitta for others. There can really be no compassion for anyone else until we have self-compassion.

However, we must be totally clear about what self-compassion actually means. "Self-compassion" or "care for the self" has become kind of a buzzword in the modern world, but how can we truly be self-compassionate? It isn't found in focusing exclusively on an individual self and catering to all its needs and expectations. It isn't in running around *doing* something to bring advantage to the self; it's in resting in ourselves as our own energy. In this way we can act clearly in terms of self-compassion and compassion for others.

We have thought that we have lost the golden thread, but now we're gathering back the golden thread that fills our heart, our body and the world. It fills them with the perfect love that is so complete. In rediscovering that golden thread, we can pour all our energy into the single feeling of love that is wisdom-exaltation, great bliss and the pure sublime essence of everything.

In the context of reification, we have been compulsive about naming everything—naming today, naming tomorrow, naming lunchtime, naming dinnertime—all these things that occur in time and space. When we hear the words "earth, water, fire, air, time, space, I, you, this and that" we would be well served to ask ourselves where the primordial sound of these words originates.

This inquiry is the beginning of truly understanding who we are. When we find the true origin of sound, things make more sense, no matter how crazed we feel our life has been. It is primordial sound, which is ever itself and which has not been made into anything.

In the West we are taught that we are *not* free in experience. We have seen our reified life as being a ping pong match between positive and negative, without ever knowing that we can be free in all experience. We can be free in the midst of the experience itself, because how could any experience give us anything or take anything away? This truth points to the teaching of freedom in immediate perception and complete perceptual openness in all experience.

We might not like someone and we might think, "I'm angry that this person has even crossed my path." However, in the context of our practice, that thought can be seen as simply an energy that has arisen and been named, but which is nothing to hold onto. This vantage means that we can be with others in an unconditional way, so that it doesn't matter what the other individual or circumstance looks like.

Whatever the situation is, we need to feel the energy that is present there, because we're within that same energy; we're part of it. So, we have a choice: we could be ruled by the thoughts and emotions, or we can instead rest as the arising energy.

Each moment has an equilibrium space. The nature of mind is the equilibrium space, the space where there is no need to effort in order to rest naturally. We're taught to make an effort, but we get to the point where "doing" and "effort" are absent, even while we're doing and efforting!

We are something so spacious and so deep, but we'll never figure that out with the reified mind. The way we truly are doesn't require figuring out, and figuring-it-out is not a recommended practice here. There's nothing "to make a figure of" in the magical display. Our life becomes complete and whole in our realization of the nature of mind, and this need not be a struggle.

❀

We need to be comfortable with our fear of the future, our regret about our past, the aspects of our lives that we usually hide from others and ourselves, and the feeling we may have that we have no one to talk to. We can find the way to simply be, whatever the emotions are, and to have the courage to share openly and honestly with others. It is so very helpful to be amongst people who can help support us. Together we find exactly who we are in the context of all our life experiences. We face things fully with our heart and mind, our heart in mind, because the heart is our mind.

We may have a kind of feeling such as, "I am completely alone. I will never be connected with anyone, and loneliness plagues me." Warmth and connection are important in human life. How generous it is to give ourselves what is really true, what is really free and what really connects us with everything. Self-generosity in each of us creates a safe space where everyone can feel accepted and embraced. There are many people in the world who feel similarly and who are also claiming this space.

If we are parents and we are contemplating the future of our children, we recognize the great need to connect with that safe space for the benefit of the children. This is a space where we realize that equalness and evenness are the case. The primordial pure space, the basic state, is not a "thing," yet, it is everything— all phenomena, whatsoever. This recognition is an aspect of an amplified human intelligence, and this is the intelligence that the future demands.

When we're in touch with our own suffering, the tremendous energy of the unconscious begins to arise with more vehemence, and the experiences brought up from the deep unconscious can be very different from anything we've ever experienced before. However, by the time something like this happens, we've already practiced enough that we can face it, and we know how to be in situations we thought we would never experience. The energy of the unconscious rises up, but now instead of trying to shut it down, we let it be.

Then there's no struggle, there's nothing to fight with, no one to fight, no birth to fight and no death to fight either. So, yes, death, there it is . . . Every single moment we're closer to death, and we don't know when death will come. Impermanence and death can be extremely frightening for people, because when we have a firmly held identity as a separate individual, death is an assault on all of the notions associated with that individuality. But with practice this changes, and when we are on our deathbed, the wisdom of the teachings will inform us. The teachings are what we need to hold close. As for myself, I practice for my deathbed.

❈

When we feel we can't practice or we're not as good as other practitioners, or we're better than the other practitioners, or whatever else it may be, it is all really meaningless. We don't have to scold ourselves for having certain thoughts about anything that is going on. We simply commit to who we truly are. We commit to the practice. This is our blessing, this cascading waterfall of nectar. So, this is the practice that our patterns and motivation have led us to. Other people are led to other practices, and each finds their place according to their pattern and motivation.

A few weeks ago, someone asked me how I was feeling, which was a surprise question in a surprise moment. The first thing I said was that I felt "fearless confidence." If you are frightened because of all that is going on in the world, you can know that you can borrow my fearless confidence, because it's limitless and not confined to one location.

Here we are all together; we are all sharing a reality that we each experience as individuals and that we experience together. We are able to go down the street loving those we meet, loving them so thoroughly and totally and without any pretense, because we really know who we are and who they are.

INCONCEIVABLE

CHAPTER TWENTY-TWO

Prior to taking on all these things from other people and from the society at large, there was—and is—something about us that is so much more profound than the conventional way we were taught to think and be.

With each short moment we are becoming educated in the true nature of mind, and with further practice the way we think changes. Our speech also changes and the way we perceive the world changes. Our heart opens up, because we are taking care of it. We can embrace others and be with them with grace and beneficial intent. This is very significant. For myself, there's certainly nothing else that has matched this, nothing at all. To me, it's inconceivable, and that's the point: it cannot be conceived of.

The gradual discovery of the nature of mind can be likened to the merging of a great river with the sea. The source of even a tremendous river is one drop of water. This one drop joins many other drops and becomes a mighty river, and it flows into the sea. Just so with practice. When the river flows into the sea, the river is no longer separate from the great ocean. This tremendous body of water is more powerful than anything that could have been imagined for the single river before the union of these waters.

We are seamless with everything. If we are seamless with everything, that means that we are abiding with everything. Everything, including us, is an everything-in-everything kind of thing.

In the West we basically know nothing about the mind. We're not trained in the nature of mind like people had been in, say for example, Tibet. From the beginning of our lives, we have been trained in reification, oppositional and causal thinking, and mere rationality. Of course, we as children didn't create this reification;

we were infants when this training began and we were gradually educated in reification all the way along.

Humans want to belong, and as a result we tend to want to act and think like the others around us so that we will be accepted. We may not think that this is the case and that we are all acting from intentional purpose, but this tendency to act according to this reified training is buried very deep in us.

If we can see things at the deepest level, we will see that, prior to taking on all these things from other people and from the society at large, there was, and is, something about us that is so much more profound than the conventional way we were taught to think and be. We really must appreciate this opportunity to engage with the practice in a very profound way.

This deeper way of being has a depth and vastness of intelligence far beyond anything that reason could ever conceive. This is the truth of it. We need this profound intelligence so very much in the world today, and we need it in a full-blown way.

❦

The suffering that we see in us and around us is profound and abundant. One way in which we suffer is that we hope for the permanence of states we like, and we hope for the dismissal of those states we don't like. However, the mind doesn't work that way. We can't choose what will arise in the mind, in case you didn't notice!

We may have felt so happy along the way that we thought the happiness would never end, but of course it always does end. Most people are probably not so naïve as I was, and they wouldn't expect unending happy states, but at one time I really bet on the happy states: "The happy states are going to win!"

But they never did win, because there is never permanence in any data stream. We have been educated in gross and subtle ways for all of our lives to believe that things are fixed and solid, so of course to see things as impermanent and lacking in an independent existence requires some inquiry and practice.

We have deeply believed in our heart of hearts that things like "I, me and mine," "others" and "the material world" exist in the way that we have taken them to be. When we believe that these things exist as separate entities, we will suffer. We have also believed that thoughts, emotions, sensations and other experiences exist as substantial entities, and in believing in this way, we suffer the results of that belief.

We need to understand that the support of a profound practice is what is required. We support ourselves like a loving parent would support a child—with kindness and a gentle and loving devotion.

The scientific perspective tells us that material reality is predominant and that cause-and-effect is the nature of things. However, science has changed repeatedly over the centuries and it is likely that it will change again. Theoretical physicists are at a breaking point in understanding material reality, and they may be in the vanguard of introducing a new way of thinking. If the new scientific perspective involves inquiry into the nature of mind, the transformation in science will be completely mind-blowing.

What if the emotions that we're naming as "an affliction" are merely misdefined; what if the name is not only inaccurate but also harmful for our well-being? These dictionary definitions are not what is true about human beings. Human beings are exalted beings, and to continue to feed humans with misdefinitions is wrong and shortsighted. The mindset that has been with us for millennia is what we're addressing in the teachings. We are now choosing a vantage that bears witness to our exaltation and compassion.

Through extending unbearable compassion to ourselves, we have the ability to genuinely extend it to others. We meditate, we practice; we meditate and we practice some more, and as we further train in it over and over again, unbearable compassion begins to be present at all times. The more familiar we are with ourselves and with our surroundings, the more comfortable we will feel, and the more comfortable we can feel extending ourselves to others.

Unbearable compassion can sound scary at first, because, well, there is that word "unbearable." After all, we typically don't want unbearable things, and we want to avoid at all costs things that might seem to be too much. When we hear about something like unbearable compassion, that can push a lot of buttons for us.

But given the track record for conventional thinking, is it not time to maybe consider things that previously seemed outrageous? These practices could be seen as esoteric or even irrational because they are beyond the scope of the conventional mind. The practices include reason and rationality, but they don't choose reason and rationality as the ultimate source of information.

Please know that you already have within you unbearable compassion. It's not anything you're hauling in from the outside. It's possible to develop confidence in unbearable compassion, because even if it does feel risky or scary, it is nourishing in a way that thinking can never be. We want to allow ourselves to dive into the unbearable compassion and deep and abiding love that are always present. It's okay to feel this love for ourselves; it isn't like we're only giving it to others without having any for ourselves.

With practice we come to the point where we do not need someone else to love us in order to experience love. In discovering the love that is fully and inherently present in ourselves, we see that the love that we have always sought is already fully in abundance within ourselves. If we do have an intimate relationship, it's no longer about what we require for ourselves; rather, it's about what we can give. The question then is, "What can I bring to the relationship to enrich my beloved?" This is done in an entirely caring and beneficial way.

❁

We have likely grown up to be very reward-oriented. Reward and punishment: "If I love someone else, they should love me," or, "If I do this thing, I will get a reward," or, "If I do that other thing, I will be punished." To be constantly thinking that we need a reward or that we could be punished for something is not an easy way to live.

So, what happens most of the time? We're suffering from the punishing thoughts that led us to seek rewards, comfort or solace, but there is so much pain in thinking that we need some kind of reward to feel better. Despite all of our efforts, most often we don't actually get a "reward"; we just end up with more names to describe what we see happening for us.

In terms of rewards, we might think, "Wow, I was hoping that meditation and practice would get me over the finish line and I'll be rid of this suffering," but there is no payoff. If we expect a payoff, we will never have one, because the idea of a payoff comes from a reliance on causal thinking. If we don't know the real purpose of meditation and practice, we may be expecting a payoff. This is what is meant by spiritual materialism: we expect a payoff or a reward. We anticipate, if not the reward of something material, maybe the reward of better thoughts and emotions or even enlightenment.

Meditation and practice aren't about a reward. They have to do with emptiness pervaded by devotional love towards oneself and towards all phenomena that have ever been, are now and will be in the future. We leave behind our wish to substantiate our own self-identity and to expand it into something we call "enlightenment." Everything about who we think we are and who we want to be needs to be set aside.

No matter how many rewards we have received and no matter how talented we are, our intrinsic worth isn't tied to the talented and rewarded self that we take ourselves to be. To identify ourselves that way would be to get totally sidetracked in reified self-identification. When we can see the absurdities in ourselves and in all of our preconceptions and misbegotten ideas, that is the beginning of humility. Humility isn't about appearing a certain way; it is not about appearances. It is the willingness to be who we truly are in relation to everyone and everything.

SELF-EDUCATING

CHAPTER TWENTY-THREE

We are born exalted! This is the power that we all have. We already are this way and so is all of what appears. There isn't anything at all that appears in our reality that is not filled chock-full with wisdom-exaltation and sublime activities.

One must see through the idea of "a personal self," because there won't be realization as long as there's focus solely on a separate self. This is absolutely key in the teachings. This is perhaps terrifying for some people to consider; nevertheless, the recognition of this must take place at some point. Some of the ancient texts mention "attachment and grasping to this life." What does that mean? It means hanging onto this individual self as though there is nothing else, and hanging on to our mind, believing that human intelligence is the only intelligence there is.

In the West, when we talk about accomplishment, we generally think about things like graduating from college, getting a good job, earning a lot of money, excelling and standing out. That is one way of living life, but is that all that we want? Are these accomplishments that are related only to causal existence the be-all and end-all in our lives? The greatest agency, authority and sovereignty are in realization, not in some kind of personal accomplishment.

Gradually through practice we realize that the attachment to an inherent existence—in which we have to prove we are someone—is loosening. When the sense of personal agency is gone beyond, what happens then? Well, we will possibly have the same things come up that we had when we thought we had a personal identity, but they will be met in an entirely different manner.

Very often people think that realization means that we get everything that we want and that all the bad and annoying things will go away, but that isn't necessarily true. Our ongoing life experience will depend on who we are and what the contributing circumstances in our lives have been.

There are things that happen in practice, negative and positive or both, so we have to be able to be humble enough to reach out for support, if needed. We cannot give what we are meant to give until we are authentic within ourselves, meaning that we keep showing up for practice and we seek the support we need.

From the very beginning we build our faith, trust, confidence and motivation to practice. How do we do that? By practicing! By hearing the teachings, contemplating their meaning and import, and practicing them. The teacher is always a practitioner too; the teacher never stops being a practitioner. Even when one goes beyond practice, there's still practice.

How do wisdom-exaltation and sublime activities come about? We have a taste of them directly when we are introduced to the nature of mind. This introduction is such a contradiction to everything we had learned before, so in that way we can see its importance right away. Once we see its importance clearly, we're emboldened to actually practice.

There's no spaciousness in being frightened of our emotions or wondering what emotion we should have or not have. It is so greatly freeing to know that the basis of the emotion is wisdom-exaltation and sublime activities.

The disease of reification and rationalism brings the disease of depression and anxiety. That's what life is when it is uninformed by the way the mind really works. But once life is informed by the way the mind really works, life becomes a natural process, because we are no longer being anything other than what we already are.

☙

Through practice we become an autodidact, which means that we self-educate ourselves to be our true selves. We learn to be with our emotions in a new way, and therein we find wisdom-exaltation and sublime activities. It doesn't mean that our particular expression is going to look exactly like the accomplished gurus we have heard about. It is helpful to know that those gurus started out the same way we did, one short moment at a time, and they had their own unique expression.

The first of the ways in which we self-educate is to turn our minds to the pith truth of the teachings. When the nature of mind teachings are first introduced, right away we're introduced to *what is*. We get a strong sense of it, and from there we practice. We get the feedback immediately because we are able to take it in. However, not everyone can take in Dzogchen teachings, actually very few. Only some practitioners can fully take in the teachings on short moments. They are the ones who had the gift of being open to that particular teaching.

Second, after turning our minds to the pith truth of the teachings, we need to practice. We practice to the degree that we can every single day. Perhaps starting out there would be one short moment, and then the next day a few short moments, but maybe the next day there are none. But by sticking with the practice we build the muscle of practice, and we become able practitioners who are educating themselves in the most skillful way.

We've been given what I feel is the greatest gift anyone could ever have. Openness to the teachings is a form of generosity, and we get what we need through openness. If we persist in the practice, we can give ourselves a little bit of encouragement by saying, "Well, I really showed up for my practice today." So, we become more and more accustomed to practice, until practice is carried on day and night. The teachings say that with continued and diligent practice there is eventually an "end to meditation." What that means is that we have gone beyond practice, but still we practice anyway.

The third aspect is removing confusion while on the path. In removing confusion, we see clearly all the reified ideas that we had been taught from the time we were born. Instead of continuing to rely on those ideas, now we are educating ourselves in a way that reveals the intelligence, wisdom-exaltation and sublime activities that are always present and available for us. I think that a good way of looking at realization is to see it as the condition of having full and unfettered access to open intelligence.

There is a purifying and transforming of confusion into pristine awareness. What does "purify" mean exactly? It means that we come to terms with ourselves as we are. "Purify" in this sense means that one becomes completely committed. With that commitment, a practitioner would want to make absolutely certain that the teachings are kept strong, and that people in the next generation will have the gifts that we have been provided.

❦

One of the best things I ever did was to listen to my gurus! Having faith and trust was immediate for me because I had been practicing the presence of God and the presence of perfect love since I was very young. I felt that, "If I'm living life this way and practicing this way, there must be someone else in the world practicing this way." There was, and when I met the gurus from Tibet, I knew that my assumption was correct.

We each have our own particular way of approaching practice, and each individual has a unique relationship with the teacher. There isn't only one kind of relationship, because we're each unique individuals, so there couldn't possibly be just one kind. If our mind is going wild and we cannot contain it, a short moment is required, and it is also important to ask the teacher to provide support. This support is especially important when we are in a state of confusion and are not able to practice.

The teachings accommodate themselves to the culture they are in, so it's much easier to understand and practice these teachings when they're in the vernacular that is used in everyday life. To understand things in very simple terms is good, because it is in fact a simple process. It may not always be easy, but it is simple.

We all have times in our life where all kinds of things can come up, and all kinds of emotionally intense things can happen that are not easy to deal with. But with a simple practice that we can rely on, we know where to turn. We want to fulfill ourselves in life and to have an opportunity to support others, and by knowing where we can turn when the going gets tough, we can do that.

In the Tibetan tradition, it is said that the greater our emotional intensity, the greater the wisdom. I am certainly one of those who was emotionally intense, and earlier on in my life I had dealt with everything with emotional intensity. I didn't really know what I was doing and I had no idea how to deal with my intense emotions other than to practice the presence of God and perfect love. Those ways of practice gave me so much.

It is very common for human beings to feel uncertain, or even frightened, about their welfare. "Will I get a good education? Am I going to find a job? Will I have a loving and attractive partner? Will we have children?" To be practicing doesn't mean that we won't participate in those things, but rather, if they do become a part of our lives, we will practice in accordance with the true energy at the basis of all things and not from descriptions based on hope, fear and doubt.

We are born exalted! This is the power that we all have. We already are this way and so is all of what appears. There isn't anything at all that appears in our reality that is not filled chock-full with wisdom-exaltation and sublime activities.

A SENSE OF DELIGHT

CHAPTER TWENTY-FOUR

When we have an opportunity to receive teachings, it is so very, very precious and wondrous. There is a sense of delight, purity, willingness to participate, and to go as deep as possible for oneself and for others for the wisdom-exaltation and enlightenment of all beings.

A teacher serves one purpose only, and that is to bring beings to realization. The teachings one receives from a teacher are the manifestation of the teacher's realization, and that same realization is being evoked in the student. Evocation is a means of communication that we may not have heard about before.

Evocation is the sharing of the teacher's heart. It is not transmission, in the sense of something being conveyed from one to another. It is the elicitation by the teacher of what is already present in the student. This sharing is a love so pure that it can never be gotten; it can only be awakened within us when we're ready for it.

When a teacher gives their teaching, it is the *sharing* of their realization; it is not just a bunch of conceptual words. When we have an opportunity to receive teachings, it is so very, very precious and wondrous. There is a sense of delight, purity, willingness to participate, and of committing as much as possible to the wisdom-exaltation and enlightenment of all beings.

Wisdom-exaltation is not the same as practical knowledge. Practical knowledge would be something like knowing what to do when the car breaks down or how to program a computer. Wisdom-exaltation on the other hand is ultimate bodhicitta coming alive and its exaltation filling all of the energies of the body. A way of thinking about wisdom-exaltation is that we have access to innumerable intelligences, and not only to the one we're operating from now. What a way to live!

We're bringing alive this great treasure in ourselves and seeing that this treasure has always existed within us, but that we did not know about it. In doing our practice, we should know that we're not in a race with ourselves or with anyone else. This is not a matter of competition. This process is also not one of humiliation; rather, it is one of humility. Humility is quite different from humiliation.

This rich humility and gratitude come from the heart. I feel humbled that I can be in this incredible Dzogchen lineage and to have had the gurus that I have had. I feel humbled because it is so rare to come into contact with a lineage and a lineage holder. It is even rarer to have a direct relationship with a guru, where one is actually in direct communication with them, as I had with Wangdor Rimpoche.

❀∽❀

The words of these teachings are probably unlike any words we've heard or read before. Just the words give us so much richness. It's a poetic expression that is unparalleled. When we connect with and benefit from these kinds of teachings, it means that we're also deeply connecting with the practitioners who have come before us.

The short moments teachings that we're receiving today are the teachings that have been received for hundreds of years. The teachings bring about realization, and so they carry all of the energy of that realization with them. The realization is in us; *it's in us*!

The short moments teachings from Tibet are hidden within other teachings. There is no book from Tibet that talks only about short moments. And why is this so? Because the gurus in Tibet taught very large groups of people, and among those individuals there were all kinds of practitioners, so the gurus' talks had to meet the needs of all the practitioners.

The short moments teachings can only have the ring of truth for people who are able to receive them. Someone else who was not ready to receive the teachings might say, "Oh, what's this?" and go right on past them. But when someone is inclined to meeting the teachings, they can recognize what the teachings are and what they mean. Those who are attracted to the teachings are then able to truly meet them in a wholehearted and vulnerable way.

We can have a practice that involves sitting for periods of times, but along with that we can be meditating in the moment with whatever we are doing. I do have a sitting meditation practice and I practice short moments in my meditation; however, for me it has become a seamless flow, so it isn't really a matter of trying to relax or trying to meditate. If we are meditating and it seems like it is not working, not to worry, that is an expression of realization too. The "work" of meditation is relaxation, not toil.

Nowadays there are many distractions, so we won't be sitting in meditation for twenty-four hours every day. Some of us have more staying power with meditation than others, but whichever way it may be for us, that is just the way it is and nothing needs to be made of it. Whatever our preference may be, we can be practicing for short moments throughout the day.

When we take a short moment, we automatically relax, open and deepen, and it isn't like we're trying to get out of ourselves. We're trying to get *into* ourselves. We want to rest in ourselves, because that's where realization is. It isn't anywhere else.

I once heard someone say, "Keep meditating even if your ass falls off." There you go. I really like that, because first of all it's a little vulgar, and second it inadvertently raises the point, "*Whose* ass is going to fall off?" I was also interested in what he meant by "meditation" in that context. I think that "keep meditating" could also be read as "keep practicing," for those who are not drawn to sitting meditation.

❀

A practitioner is spared the bitter experience of someone who is just trying to make it through life relying on reified thinking and who is trying to ignore suffering through engaging in all kinds of distracting activities. It is very important in our practice to come to the point of really feeling the suffering in the world and knowing fully the intensity and immensity of the suffering of beings, and how best to respond to it.

We can practice fully in the midst of whatever life is bringing us; there's nowhere else to go. It isn't like, "Oh gosh, I'm having all these thoughts, and there is nothing I can do about it and I need to get out of this." It's about resting in whatever it is we're thinking, feeling or experiencing. We're not trying to make that-which-is into something else. Instead, we're practicing as has been taught. We're practicing short moments.

Human beings, as we know, have an inclination to do all kinds of things, so we never know what's going to happen in the world. All kinds of craziness can occur, so we have to be clear about what to do when there's some kind of upset or something adverse that is happening. We can play our part in securing the teachings, supporting people who are open to them and skillfully dealing with all the turmoil.

Some of the current world events have brought up a lot of fear in people, which is, as with all the afflictive emotions, something to rest in. By practicing—by practicing a lot—we become able to rest even in the most disturbing states. Indeed, we are able to deal with and handle something as powerful as extreme fear.

I really have a very simple disposition, even though it may sound like I don't. I like a teaching that is simple enough so that the message gets across, but no simpler than that. We have to know that balancing point for ourselves: an expression that is simple and not elaborate or complicated, but no simpler than is necessary to deal with these sorts of disturbing states.

❈

Impartiality is one of the aspects of realization. It doesn't mean we don't express ourselves in life in one or the other of the oppositional ways, because we live in the context of causality. However, if we practice rationalism along with causal and binary thinking, we will look at things one way, but if we practice Dzogchen, we see things from an entirely different vantage.

The realization in this practice brings us to the point of impartiality. However, "impartial" doesn't mean deadened or indifferent. Impartial means a refusal to create a conflict between good and bad, happy or sad, advantageous or non-advantageous or any of the other opposites. There is no longer an enslavement to the pairs of opposites; that's what impartial means.

The most skilled response comes from tranquility, and it's very clear whether tranquility is present or not. If we feel anger, even a little tiny irritation or annoyance, we don't try to get away from it, but immediately rest as it.

The realization of Dzogchen is tranquil, but that doesn't mean that we just sit around all blissed out and do nothing. It means that no matter what we do or express, it comes from tranquility and compassion. The response does not come from anger, revenge, hatred or from some other such thing. Even if there are wrathful skillful means being employed, it is clear that they are coming from tranquility and compassion.

To the degree that one can practice tonglen, it is essential to practice, as tonglen delivers incredible results. Another reason why it's important to practice tonglen is that, for most of us, compassion wasn't part of our training or upbringing, but when we practice it, we're providing loving benefit to those who are suffering. Most of us have not known that we have—we are—the essential nature of compassion. When we hear about it, it sparks a recognition, and we remember. Thus, tonglen, the receiving of suffering and the giving of compassion, is an ideal practice to spark that remembrance.

Utter bodhicitta—utter compassion—is what is called buddha-nature, the substratum of everything, the unconditioned, abiding nature of reality. The pink lotus of bodhicitta grows in the mud, arises from the mud and opens to the world without even a single speck of mud. This is why it is a symbol of ultimate bodhicitta.

Section Four:

SHOWING UP FULLY

25. The Desire for Experience   160

26. Generosity   165

27. The Union of Opposites   170

28. Showing Up   175

29. Workability   181

30. Unbidden and Non-Grasping Love   187

31. A Life of Exciting Mystery   194

32. The Ultimate Solution   200

THE DESIRE FOR EXPERIENCE
CHAPTER TWENTY-FIVE

Instead of being intoxicated with experience, we need to be intoxicated with love, a love that goes beyond all understanding. Love in the end is connected with the energy we feel within ourselves, and this energy carries a profundity of love that is unknowable and inconceivable.

As all experiences are impermanent and thereby ultimately unsatisfactory, the pursuit of the desire for experience is based on a fundamental misunderstanding of the nature of reality. It is a delusion to believe that we can find essential happiness and fulfillment only through the outer experiences that we have.

The desire for experience is based on a false sense of self. We believe that we are separate and independent beings, but this is an illusion. In reality, all of existence is interconnected and interdependent. When we cling to the illusion of a separate self, we create suffering for ourselves and others.

From this belief in the independent existence of things, the desire for experience arises. The energy of reified and causal perception is used to describe things—as positive or negative, good or bad— and this initial impulse to describe, and then covet or reject, could be said to be what prompts the desire for experience.

We seek experiences—relationships, acquisitions, success— believing that these will bring fulfillment, and we can become intoxicated by this desire for experience. While experiences can bring temporary satisfaction, the satisfaction is impermanent, and attachment to the experiences leads to suffering when they fade or fail to fully satisfy.

We go from one experience to another without experiencing lasting joy in an ongoing way. Because we have been trained up in the desire for experience and have known only this in the context of the culture in which we live, we often don't know that there is another way to be. We bounce around from one experience to the other without ever realizing the trap that we are in.

❦

This is all due to the reification that tells us that if we attain enough experiences, then everything will be all right. We think that if we just have the experiences we want and nothing but that, we will be happy, but sadly we find this to be a misguided wish. Once we do indeed come to see that the desire for experience leads to dissatisfaction, this can have a very profound effect.

Once we recognize the cycle of unhappiness—wanting, and then getting, but not being satisfied, or wanting more but not getting it, repeated over and over again—the desire for experience seems a lot less compelling. If we are very fortunate, at some point we come to see that we don't want any longer to live in a way where we're constantly seeking novelty and more stimulation. We see that we can't get the fundamental satisfaction we crave if we continue to seek satisfaction only in the experiences.

The desire for experience is very strong. We wander aimlessly and experience suffering because of the tight grip of the reification of experience. A way forward to the decisive realization of the nature of the desire for experience is through the practice of short moments, repeated many times, with patience and resolve, until the short moments become spontaneous.

The ability to see the desire for experience without being overwhelmed by it comes through proper understanding, determination and strength of heart. Our responsibility and commitment is to rest, and to rest completely as whatever it is that comes up. That's the way we can come to see ourselves and everything else *as it is*.

Instead of being intoxicated with experience, we need to be intoxicated with love, a love that goes beyond all understanding. Love in the end is connected with the energy we feel within ourselves, and this energy carries a profundity of love that is unknowable and inconceivable.

Another term for false perceptions is "ignorance," as it is called in Dzogchen. Ignorance isn't a simple lack of knowledge, but rather a fundamental misunderstanding of reality. It is a matter of being trapped by causal thinking and by the belief that having the desired experiences will lead to fulfillment.

What we might have considered as "fact" from this vantage is simply fascinated attention. Fascinated attention! If we examine each of the constructs that we've held, we begin to see that there is something vitally more important than the data streams we've had and all the information that we've allowed to define ourselves, and which have led us into increasing desire for experience.

Ignorance prevents us from seeing beyond the constant craving for more. In our practice, this fundamental ignorance needs to be investigated and challenged. We come to see that, as long as we rely only on causal ideas, we are in denial and there is little motivation to go beyond the desire for experience.

In order to understand the desire for experience, we need to know how it came about. First, we have to come to the inquiry: "If I could get out of this trap of being overwhelmed by emotional states and all my thoughts and longings, what would that be like?" Fortunately, when we're introduced to Dzogchen, the relief we feel in that introduction is already evident and we are led to find answers to our questions.

When we examine our desire for experience, we see that it is connected to our actions and their outcomes; therefore, it is important to understand the nature of our actions. The action is to try to fulfill ongoing desires, and the result is to suffer.

In confronting the suffering in a direct way, in knowing what suffering is and what impermanence is, in reflecting on the profound meaning of these and their importance to practice, decisive realization and pure perception become more available to us. When we fundamentally understand impermanence, we loosen the desire for experience, because we can see the transience of all things. Understanding that everything is fleeting helps us to see the futility of clinging to experiences.

Maybe even more importantly, we understand clearly that death will come. Initially, the purpose of the Dzogchen teachings was to train people to die well. To know how to die well is very important, and in reflecting on death, we reflect on impermanence in life and the nature of the desire for experience.

❁

It would be an extreme to say that all desires are "harmful," for how could one lead an embodied existence without the desire to maintain that body? In the practice of Dzogchen, one does not reject the desire for experience, but engages wisely with it. One sees clearly what causes pain and dissatisfaction. Neither indulgence nor extreme renunciation is the path; instead, one cultivates being fully aware in each experience, accepting both pleasure and pain, happiness and sadness, with equanimity and balance. One engages with experiences in a way that fosters insight, compassion, and wisdom rather than attachment.

The causal domain—the realm of cause and effect that we perceive with the senses and that is the context for the desire for experience—is so tiny as to almost be invisible in relation to all the other intelligences that exist. The causal domain only operates within a minuscule domain. Let's say that the intelligence of the universe is made up of millions of puzzle pieces. In that case, the causal domain would be only one piece, and not the entirety.

The causal domain has no power outside of its own purview and can only address causal issues. But what about all the other millions of "puzzle pieces"? Is there something implied here that could lead us to inquire into a knowledge that reflects our actual reality? It is possible that our survival as a human species will depend on being able to broaden out from one puzzle piece to looking at things in a much more comprehensive way.

The more that this comprehensive vantage occurs, the more wisdom will be revealed. It isn't like we have to get to a certain point in time in order to have the reign of shining wisdom. Wisdom is the soothing energy of everything, and we already have this energy within us to spontaneously respond to the circumstances at hand. Wisdom has the ability to know things in their totality, and also to know things specifically.

We no longer need to follow a causal path in dealing with the desire for experience. We also no longer need to figure out how one causal event is related to another. We are not building knowledge; we are discovering knowledge that is already present. We don't have to depend on an outline of how we are going to do something; we function in vulnerability and in the spontaneity of knowledge in each moment.

GENEROSITY

CHAPTER TWENTY-SIX

Instead of approaching others through competition or seduction, we approach them with generosity. "I only want to understand you. I'm here to give to you."

One could say that one of the most radiant gems of practice is generosity. Generosity is one of the signs of accomplishment and contains all other virtues. The heart essence is generous; it is giving itself at all times. Generous energy is always profound. We are being generous by being committed to short moments of peace and compassion, and every short moment expressed in that way is a very precious gift to all beings. We practice for ourselves and our own edification and illumination, but we also practice for the benefit of all, the enlightenment of all, the basic sanity of all, the good cheer of all.

To be generous with every aspect of our mind, speech and body fills us with affection and kindness—towards ourselves initially—but this naturally extends to others as well. Boundless, unfettered, outrageous large-heartedness doesn't need proof that someone is worthy to receive generosity.

It is said in Dzogchen that the highest form of generosity is to share the teachings with others. Openness to the teachings in a person to whom the teachings are being offered is also a form of generosity. What could be a greater gift than to generously share the profound love that has been given to us in the form of the teachings? However, even if we were to receive the greatest teachings in the world, if we didn't practice, we would get the results of non-practice.

Profound generosity is the impulse to give to others and to be generous at heart, knowing the effect this can have on the people we come into contact with. The practice of generosity can lead to a true sense of connection with other beings, where there may have been very little before. Instead of approaching others through competition or seduction, we approach them with generosity. "I only want to understand you. I'm here to give to you." That's a much different approach compared to what most folks are accustomed to. Often people really feel the kindness and appreciate it.

In life we face all kinds of circumstances, and some of them are very challenging. It may seem overwhelming to be gentle, affectionate, amiable and generous to someone who is extremely disruptive to our life. However, no matter how intense the energy is that comes up for us in regard to that person, through rest and settledness it's possible to recognize it as our native energy, rather than moving into aggression with a driving passion to get even.

Throughout our lives our energy has been developed and described in a certain way, but it can be redeveloped and looked at in a new way. We practice, and we can see this energy as vast. It's vast like the sky and deep like the sea. It is present within us and in everything we know and see. This is something that can only be realized; it can't be understood through causal ideas.

⊜∞⊜

Hooray for all of our personal challenges, as well as the many daunting global issues! Well, why "hooray"? Because it is these very pressing concerns that are evoking in us the urge to seek solutions. Due to the prolific engagement online around the world, people now are becoming more and more aware of the negative emotions that were once kept secret. These negative opinions and activities were not shared with anyone before the online world brought them right into our living rooms.

In social media we find every possible emotion and belief, as well as opinions beyond what we ever thought possible for people to believe or express. This can seem very frightening in a certain way. However, we can see from the vantage of being practitioners that what is occurring brings the suffering of the world into full display, no matter what form it is taking, and no matter how horrifying it is. When suffering becomes so obvious, some generous people are moved to find the path beyond suffering for themselves and others.

There is a great deal of generosity in being able to understand the suffering others are experiencing, but then also to be able to enter into true love with them with no resistance. By overcoming the initial resistance or antipathy that may arise, we can understand the energies and know what came about for the person, why it came about and how it has unfolded for them.

There is a brief practice that extends our generosity out into the world. It's similar to tonglen in a way and has three parts: the first one entails bringing to mind a person toward whom we already feel affection. We relate to the hardship the person has had in their life and how they have been able to handle it or not handle it.

To directly see that someone you know and care about is suffering sparks compassion. That's a way of connecting your energy with a person and to acknowledge the suffering that is occurring for them. We wish for them self-affection and self-love and that they can be free of anxiety and pain.

The next part of the practice is to feel love and devotion for someone we know, but whom we don't know well. We wish that they would be able to be happy and to have their suffering resolved. We wish for the person everything that we with all of our life force have to provide.

When we feel our life force going from our own body—that we have felt for so long belonged only to us—to "another," that distance from "myself" to "another" is bridged. When we extend our whole life force to someone else, giving them everything that we have realized, we come to see that "our" life force is everywhere. It isn't ours personally. It is the life force of everything that is.

The final stage is to contribute our generous offering to someone we feel animosity towards. Maybe we don't even feel animosity, but we resent them and don't want them around. They could be exhibiting hostility towards us, and that can be a lot for us to deal with. It causes a strong negative vibe for us, and it feels like the strong vibe could slip into hatred and violence. So, for sure, that is a challenging situation to be in.

But once again, as before, we allow the loving and beneficial energy to flow towards them. That other person actually has the same energy we do; it's just being described and acted on by them in a different way. But we have to know what to do in this situation. We look at everything going on and then decide what would be good for everyone. We set up a compassionate field, as it were, and act skillfully.

With practice, we begin to realize the softness and expansiveness of this energy. Our intelligence is soft and always present. As this soft intelligence, we are always living and subsuming notions like life and death, good and bad, rational and irrational. Any hard-edged description that presents itself as being in opposition to another hard-edged description is probably not a motivating force we want to follow.

Instead, we leave all these interpretations and we rest, and soon we begin to see the ways in which these hard-edged descriptions have affected our whole life and our interpretation of what it means to be human. We really want to get in touch with this and realize the origin of everything that seems to be produced from outside or that is self-produced. Regardless of its description, it is the softness of primordial intelligence.

As we can see nowadays in society and online, there is a ramping up of negative data streams. It is as though every negative thing anyone has ever thought and all the negative energy that ever has been is coming to light. Instead of being carried away by all of the obvious negativity, we remain as the space that does not provoke and that does not engage in negative and harmful activity.

It's not okay to be abused, but at the same time it is possible to rest and to respond skillfully from the vantage of benefit, and we can better understand what is going on in this particular afflictive setting. Instead of demonizing those who disagree with us or who criticize us, we can see the abusers as a human being. That's what workability means: to turn the abuse around and to playfully reshape it in the way that a child would shape clay into something new. When we rest profoundly, we find that the turmoil that has so filled our minds begins to clear up.

If we say, "Oh, this feels uncomfortable," then we're naming that energy that feels negative to us. This is a perfect time to rest completely as the energy of everything that is, which is all that we are. Nothing is inherently positive or negative. We rest as always-on profundity, the intelligence that subsumes the causal definitions of positive and negative. What a generous gift to give to ourselves.

THE UNION OF OPPOSITES

CHAPTER TWENTY-SEVEN

In the beginning, the full recognition of equalness and evenness may sound remote, but as we move along, we reach a point where we can think about the world in those terms. Yes, the union of opposites: very powerful realizations coming about spontaneously free of conventional limitations and definitions.

It is such a great gift to be able to inquire into things and to try to understand what is happening in our lives. It is always good to ask, "What is ultimately real and true?" That inquiry can lead us to a deeper insight into what is occurring. As this inquiry bears more and more fruit, at some point it becomes spontaneous and goes on without prompting or effort. We experience the genuine self in the deeper realization of our energy.

The powerful energy in us is connected to the energy of all. This energy is the intelligence through which we perceive ourselves and through which we perceive everything else. At first we may start to understand it just a bit, and then we have the first blink of instinctive recognition.

In moving beyond the realm of normal perception, we would no longer be only seeing the projections of things. For instance, when we see a tree or any other object, what we think we are seeing is merely a projection, like a mirage. In a certain way it is what we have been trained to see, and through that training what we expect to see.

Whatever these images may be, they're all energy, but when we only address them in a conventional way, our understanding is limited. As scary as it might be initially, we need to thoroughly investigate our previously held assumptions, and we rest while doing so. The more we rest, the more we are gifted with complete perceptual openness and freedom in immediate perception.

When we feel our own energy, it's much easier to feel a connection with all. Say we're at home all alone with our little kitty cat and we feel so lonely and that nobody likes us, and we think, "Oh, woe is me." Well, that's one idea about things, but what is really going on? If people in that state of mind can rest in the energy of themselves, they can come to know the heart connection that connects all things. Where is the loneliness then?

In the Dzogchen teachings, what we have known as "emotions" are in fact profound wisdom, and through practice we can come to know them as such. It's a matter of resting in our energy and growing familiar with ourselves as an energy system, which is what we always are. This energy is an intelligence; it is intelligence. We call it open intelligence, and it is also deep intelligence.

Our perception that we are a separate individual is based only on what we have learned throughout our lives. If I say, "I am somebody," that occurs in one moment, but in the next moment our attention is somewhere else. If we really reflect, we can see that we are rarely focused on ourselves ongoingly as being "somebody." Most often we are simply the flow of life, and this is the way it actually is: that we are a flow of energy and are never a concrete thing. It is only that we have been trained to believe that we are a concrete personality.

❧⊱⊰❧

When appropriate practices are adopted, apparently confusing teachings such as "the union of opposites" or "the equalness and evenness of love and hate" are easier to understand. In the beginning, the full recognition of equalness and evenness may sound remote, but as we move along, we reach a point where we can think about the world in those terms. Yes, the union of opposites: very powerful realizations coming about spontaneously free of conventional limitations and definitions.

These are teachings for how beings are living *now*, and not in the distant past. For our Western culture, an idea like "the union of opposites" is an unfamiliar way of understanding things; however, I feel that as we move forward there will be many more practitioners who will have the direct realization of the union of opposites.

When we rest fully, we come to know the no-experience part of an experience, and that is once again the union of opposites. In doing so, we experience the energy *as it is*. That's it, with no commentary or thinking required. As we do so, we feel more and more united with all experience, and we find that the realization is not only open, but that it is also endlessly deep. We enter into this depth when we rest in the energy in our body. The great depth in ourselves is experienced directly.

The energy of emotions is not our enemy. Sometimes emotions are so powerful that we just want to get rid of them, and we devise all kinds of antidotes to free ourselves from them. However, the most important way of being is to rest in the energy. We can forget everything else that we have learned about the emotions, because resting in the energy shows directly what wisdom-energy is like.

We come to understand that these energies—the pacifying, magnetizing, wrathful energies, or whatever they might be—are profound wisdom. At first the energy feels entirely new, but that is where we rest: in that energy.

The energies are much easier to understand, recognize and realize when they are felt instinctively. "Instinctive" is then no longer only an abstraction. We begin to *feel* the energy, and we rest in it. If it's an energy that has formerly made us sad or led us to go wild or whatever it is, now we can rest in it, honor it and know that it is the energy of profound wisdom.

When we rest in the energy, it's much easier to feel the connection with all beings and to practice tonglen. We might even practice tonglen with a person we don't like! We feel the energy of not liking the person, but then also the wish to reach out, even if the person would never, ever, care to have anything to do with us. We give all of our benevolent energy to that person and take in their pain and suffering. Why? Because we can.

We may have not only disliked that person, but we may even have hated them, but now there is the wish to take away their pain and suffering. Tonglen is about resting in these powerful energies. We can visualize that through sharing the compassionate energy, the pain is being taken away from both the person practicing tonglen and the person who is receiving the loving radiance of tonglen.

Imagine not liking someone but then using the energy to reach out in love to them and taking away their pain. It might feel uncomfortable at first. "Why would I want to take anyone else's pain, and especially with this person, when I have so much pain of my own?" It doesn't seem like that could possibly work and that it would only cause us to accumulate more suffering. But that isn't the case. In fact, we grow stronger each time we practice.

As we progress in the practice, we can incorporate more beings into our tonglen meditation, until we reach the point that we can take the suffering of all beings into ourselves and give only goodness. This is a very beautiful way to go about life. It is greatly connecting and powerful to really get the *feeling* of being. As we become familiar with energy in our own body, we feel more and more like we are soaring. At the same time, we have incredible grounded-ness and connection with everything that is, rather than maybe only with a few familiar people.

❀

The world no longer exists in the same way it did prior to the pandemic. I feel much greater unity among all people and much more of a commitment to beings and to the planet, Mother Earth, which is what we are. We are Mother Earth; we're like bits of Mother Earth walking around!

I can thank the pandemic for having really elevated the importance of people unifying with one another to conquer a common problem. I feel the pandemic has brought forth an appreciation for all beings in a new way. It has secured a culture of benevolence in a time when people are beginning to have their eyes opened.

Human beings have not connected like this before. Just to feel the energy and the excitement of that—*Wow*! We have an opportunity to give to others what is being provided to us by the teachings. We have the opportunity to benefit beings in a very direct way, because more and more humans are opening up to new possibilities.

The ideas of the past are fading away, and as practitioners we can step up to serve in a very direct and profound way. It is a matter of understanding the ideas and needs people have and providing teachings according to where people are. We take up the mantle of faith and trust, and we have a motivation to offer teachings that are of benefit to beings everywhere.

SHOWING UP

CHAPTER TWENTY-EIGHT

One could describe "practice" as showing up wholeheartedly for the teachings. As we practice short moments, each short moment is a golden drop of insight that never goes away, because that insight is a reflection of truth, of reality, of natural mind.

Once we have received an authentic introduction to open intelligence, it's very important to practice short moments as often as possible throughout the day. In the beginning, it might not be so easy, but it could be. We must keep our motivation to practice alive. If we stop practicing for any reason, it only takes one short moment to start again.

One could describe "practice" as showing up wholeheartedly for the teachings. As we practice short moments, each short moment is a golden drop of insight that never goes away, because that insight is a reflection of truth, of reality, of natural mind. That is what is happening, and we can acknowledge that for ourselves.

By listening to, thinking about and meditating on the teachings, we intentionally transform our vantage in life through the warmth we feel in ourselves. If we think a kind thought or a not-so-kind thought about someone, in practice both warm us, and we can feel the warmth of that energy in our body—warm, warm, warm.

We gather up all the joys and sorrows and all the individuals that we might feel disconnected from for some reason, and we draw all this together into a great celebration. So, imagine all the people you've ever thought about in a negative way, and there you are celebrating with them in the relief that comes from genuine compassion.

⊜∞⊜

Just as there are people from many lands, there are people of many minds. Every single human being is unique and has a mind of their own. However, that "mind of their own" is the expression of an intelligence that is never truly separated out into individual minds.

There can be a lot of energy that arises for us in response to hateful remarks we receive from others, but it doesn't mean we have to be reactive. When the anger and resistance press on us in any way, we can keep practicing. When a word of anger or resistance occurs in the mind, it comes from primordial sound. It's important at the moment one feels the negative energy to rest profoundly as the sound.

What has been hurled at us is another person's view, not our view. Theirs could be a common view and accepted manner of speaking, but if we take it on ourselves, it then becomes common to us. We can rest as the power of who we are, and there is no limit in that. In this way we show up fully, and we will not be engulfed by the common view.

We surely cannot control what other people say or do. We may hope that they will change, but I learned long ago that the hope that a person will change is a very limiting space to live from. What we need to rely on is our power, and not on hope. We can commit to our power in solving problems and dealing with situations. The more we get in touch with our energy and power, the easier it is to be skillfully present in each situation.

There are so many beautiful things in life. If we look with eyes of sublime knowledge, we see a beauty that can never be taken away. When we look at another person, whether their intent is the best intent or the worst, every single one of those people has the same inherent human dignity.

People can do all kinds of things, just like each one of us has and will, and yet, at our basis we have human dignity. Whether we're doing the best thing or the worst thing in the world, it does not change the fact of our fundamental dignity. An easy way to maintain compassion is to remember human dignity. Even though we perhaps learned something else, we always are in essence this fundamental dignity.

It's important to be bold and to face everything and avoid nothing—again, to face everything and avoid nothing. Each person is already who they truly are, and there's no way to take that reality away. We remain open, come what may, and we attract what we're open to. We remain fully alive and open to the miracles that are possible.

🔔

I learned something from my guru, Wangdor Rimpoche, that I think is so precious and sacred, which is that no matter what anyone is doing, they are doing it because of their life pattern—their karma. It is very, very important for us to recall the fact that if we had the same data as someone else, we would be doing exactly the same things they are doing. The only way that we can befriend them is to be in there with them totally and to have empathy, compassion and bodhicitta.

I feel so very blessed and fortunate to have my life. If I told you everything about my life and all the things that have gone on, I think you might say, "I for sure don't want that life!" We each have to contend with ourselves exactly as we are and our life exactly as it is. However, the thing we need to be most concerned with is the brilliance of our inherent open intelligence.

If I would have seen my life today from the perspective of fifty years ago, I would have had no idea of how I could have made it from there to here. None. And then to feel like I feel today—to feel so whole and that my life had value before and has value now, well, none of this would have happened for me without resting, and I know it.

With each step of the way and each bit of insight, I feel like the most fortunate person on earth, I really do. I wonder how in the world my life could ever be this way. How could this happen to me? How could it be that I would be here after feeling so distraught and overwhelmed earlier in my life, and yet come out whole? How does that happen? Because that wholeness is native to us; that's how it happens.

It's up to us to give ourselves unbearable compassion. To practice unbearable compassion means facing everything and avoiding nothing, and that is what we're working towards in the practice.

☙

Just as there were specifically Tibetan capacities within the unique Tibetan culture, we also have our own capacities to face the challenges we are facing. There are possibilities for the teachings around the globe in this era which do not look like the Tibetan teachings. We don't know exactly how things in the world will unfold, but we can continue to show up and to offer the teachings in the most beneficial way possible.

Dzogchen wasn't practiced by large numbers of people in its Tibetan setting, but many of those who did practice became enlightened. The fact that even one person was enlightened gives us hope, because if there's even one, then we also have the opportunity. In certain circumstances there might not be any examples of enlightenment around us, and yet we still have the opportunity.

I find this Dzogchen teaching to be of such significance that I really don't have the words for it. It is so very, very important. There are amazing things happening today around the globe and there are incredible people around the world who are contributing in incredible ways. These moments of authentic engagement are of urgent necessity. We are carrying something precious into the world.

❈

Every single manifestation is illusory and self-releasing, and every here-and-now is entirely self-releasing without anyone ever doing anything. Wow, we're dealing with a very profound intelligence in that single statement! Something that is totally illusory—though it seems to appear—never actually appears in the way we take it to be. To gain this magnificent insight is why we practice.

It is so important to take advantage of our precious human birth and the opportunity it affords us to discover the sublime endowments that we have within us. When we practice, we meet ourselves as we are, which is a way of being that we likely did not know before. For instance, we have had no idea that our mind is meant to be calm and powerful regardless of what is occurring. It doesn't matter what the thought is or what the physical or emotional struggle is, we always remain as we truly are, regardless.

Our purpose is very great, even though we might feel that we are very small. Maybe none of you feel small, but from what I've observed in my many years, this feeling of inadequacy does come up strongly for many people. Whatever our opinion about ourselves has been, now we're meeting a new friend, a new way of thinking and being, and that friend has a single face.

I really encourage you, to whatever degree is possible, to speak your truth in a gentle, firm and confident way—first to yourself— so that you feel as strong as you are meant to be, and to give yourself everything. *Give yourself everything that is already yours.*

There are difficult things that happen in life, so we have to be able to be humble enough to reach out for support, if needed. We cannot give what we are meant to give until we are authentic within ourselves, meaning that we keep showing up for practice and we seek the support we need.

The longer that I'm on this earth breathing in and out, the more I see the importance of realizing reality-nature. The way we've been taught to treat ourselves in a reified life is so sad. The recognition of this sadness allows the capacity to understand the unbearable suffering of beings. When we engage with the suffering of the world, we do so from the place of unbearable compassion, and this is where the exaltation of wisdom and the great bliss of sublime activities occur.

WORKABILITY

CHAPTER TWENTY-NINE

I love looking for workability, especially when I have no idea what to do. I just wait, and pretty soon the package comes fully wrapped and ready to go!

Once we are introduced to open intelligence, we may not even know what it is we've been introduced to. But because of our motivation and sincerity, we are open to the teachings, and then along the way some trust comes. As we practice further, faith and confidence develop, and through the faith and confidence the teachings give us more and more insight and capacity.

As we practice more, we will begin to see the results, and as we practice still more, we can see where we might need to practice a little bit more. In the course of our lives there will be things that come up that will press us in one way or another, and there is no human being alive who does not experience challenging circumstances. However, there is a distinction between acting out based on thoughts and emotions, as opposed to responding to the thoughts and emotions based on wisdom energy.

Yes, life can be very difficult and challenging, and it is more and more so for people all over the world. I think what is needed right now is for us to be very discerning about what is important at this time in the world. We want to be clear about what has supported us to get where we are now and what can provide for the future. I don't want to suffer, and I don't want my children, grandchildren or great grandchildren to suffer. I don't want all this suffering for my brothers and sisters, my friends, my sangha or the world as a whole. What is a possible solution?

I feel that the Dzogchen teachings on workability are very, very important. Before I heard about the teachings, I tended to shy away from some disturbing things in my life because I considered them unworkable. They were not workable because I did not know how to look for the workability.

Regardless of the situation we are facing, it is workable, and now I love looking for workability, especially when I have no idea what to do. I just wait, and pretty soon the package comes fully wrapped and ready to go! It's such a glorious gift. Who would want to reject this gift? Certainly, I wouldn't, and I know that you wouldn't either.

The principle of workability is essential to compassion, because when we understand through our resting practice the principle of workability, compassion becomes very clear. After all, these are teachings that make our own life workable and place us in a vantage of non-worry and non-concern, and from this basis we can reach out to others. It may be a situation that we didn't ask for, and it may be one that is dire, dangerous and threatening, but the workability in it is found through a wise and skillful response.

❀⊙❀

When we only practice binary thinking, we only have an illusory idea of what is real. The culture in which we have grown up did not know how to train us in the nature of our mind. We have been taught to name our energies incorrectly, and we have been trained in binary thinking, which, despite what we may have learned, isn't the only aspect of intelligence.

Binary thinking is a very limited domain of intelligence; however, we as human beings have access to countless intelligences and to a vast menu of teachings from which we can choose. Once the binary mind we have trained in becomes obvious to us, we can say, "Wow, I think I can do something about this. Maybe things can be handled another way."

For all of my life the most important thing has been to discover the nature of mind. Just like we each develop our interests from the time we are very young, this happened to be mine. But when we don't feel understood or we feel ignored, that can bring up all kinds of things. For me it brought up a lot of aggression, and I thought, "What do I do with this aggression? How do I get rid of it?"

I was trained in the way that, "If you don't like it, get rid of it." In the end though, there's nothing to get to, nowhere to go and nothing to get rid of. It's simply a matter of realizing this. Basic okay-ness, basic sanity is our prize. This is what we have within us, and nothing can disrupt it.

In our culture, aggression is very common, and when the energy of aggression appears, "aggression" is what we imagine the energy to be. But when we rest with that energy without naming it, there is an opportunity to see it *as it is*. Anger and aggression are mislabeled, because in actual fact they are wisdom. Through clear-light wisdom we see everything *as it is*, and more and more this comes about spontaneously.

We can often tell what an emotion is from the effect that goes with it. If it is love, then we feel it; it reaches our heart and we feel the warmth. If it's a harmful view, the effect is disruptive and disturbing, and the energy in our body tells us that. When we pay attention to our energy and see it for what it truly is, it shares its story of exaltation and sublimity. Exaltation and sublimity are our very own right now.

In continuing with the resting practice, we begin to be more aware of this energy that is in us. When we're resting, we aren't spaced out and somewhere else; we're resting devotedly as the energy in our body. This energy in which we are resting is the luminous intelligence that pervades emptiness. We can rest mightily in this understanding and enjoy love and bliss in a way we haven't before. When we can truly feel the energies in the body, we feel something that is similar to maternal warmth. The intention is to have this generous energy of maternal warmth be always-on as the flow of compassion.

Regardless of what our cognitive processing might be involved in, the bottom line is compassion—bodhicitta. That's the practice here: compassion, but also unbearable compassion. When we rest, we are giving ourselves unbearable compassion. Even though the word "unbearable" with compassion may be new to us, nevertheless, it gets our attention, because we probably hadn't heard it used that way before.

I am drawn to compassion and now I am equally drawn to unbearability, and I think that it is a great adjective to add to compassion. Unbearable compassion is the greatest gift any of us can ever receive, and it is our greatest gift to give. What a way to live. When I began reflecting on unbearable compassion and began practicing it, I found it to be like drinking a nectar of love.

❁

In a very practical way, we need to find our wisdom nature, and then through that discovery, we begin to describe our experience in accordance with our wisdom nature, instead of describing things through binary thinking, as we have done before. I feel very blessed that we have found what we are looking for in this wisdom teaching. No one can take this treasure away from us.

Simply stated, wisdom is learning how to be and to act wisely. When we talk about Dzogchen, we are talking about wisdom-exaltation and sublime activities that are expressions of practical, everyday wisdom. The solutions to the crises in the world are available, but not through binary thinking. Binary thinking never really solves the problems, because binary thinking is not sourced in wisdom.

There have been times in human history when there have been inconceivable challenges; however, we as a human species were able to survive those challenges. Even with all of what we are facing in the present day, we can look at what is going on, and we figure out the variables and find some kind of solution. It's just that with the Dzogchen practice, the solutions are coming from a different place, a place of wisdom, and they're much more powerful.

As the teachings spread around the world, they need to match the culture in which they are being offered. We're in a global culture now, so we need to have simplified terms that can reach everyone and which can lead to the resolution of the problems we are facing. I know for certain that wisdom has much better solutions when compared to the solutions offered by binary thinking, and I know that wisdom arrives at bold and sparkling conclusions, such that problems that seemed overwhelming before no longer are so.

Wisdom-insight is clearly unique when compared to any other kind of intelligence. When we rest, we're resting as this wisdom energy. As we continue to rest, we become more and more familiar with it. That's why my guru, Wangdor Rimpoche, said probably hundreds of times, "Just keep meditating," which can also be expressed as, "Just keep practicing."

❁

When we have an explosion of all kinds of things that we do not want in our lives, that's a great time to practice. There are so many riches there. It might seem like, "Oh gosh, I don't know if I can practice another minute, this is so overwhelming," and all kinds of other things. However, we stay with it, no matter what our editorial comment is. As Wangdor Rimpoche said, we keep meditating. And at the same time, it is very important to know what exactly we are "meditating" on.

In terms of "meditating," I love his story about a monk and his yak. The monk was totally obsessed with the yak and he couldn't stop thinking about it. The yak was his only focus, to the exclusion of all else, and so eventually the story goes that as a result of his deep meditation on the yak, he turned into a yak! Rinpoche said, "It's really important to keep meditating (practicing). If you keep meditating on the yak, then you'll get the yak. If you keep meditating on your true nature, you will receive the gifts that come from that focus."

Wisdom is great love and great bliss. The energy in our body is wisdom energy. It is completely loving and completely blissful one hundred percent of the time. The coupling of great love and great bliss is what Dzogchen is. It constitutes loving, blissful, always-present wisdom-energy.

I believe that people want to love and be loved, and we are always looking for love, but often do not actually know what we're looking for. When we rest, we are resting as the loving, blissful energy that is our own. All the energy that we are, have been or will be is here right now.

UNBIDDEN AND NON-GRASPING LOVE

CHAPTER THIRTY

Through the practice we find a love we didn't know was possible. This is the love that belongs to open intelligence. It is an uncontrived, non-grasping love that is unbidden. It is something we did not make up with our mind, as in, "I will love this person if they love me."

We all have troubles, and we all have times when things are completely out of control, especially if we're practitioners. Why is this sometimes especially so for practitioners? Because practitioners are able to notice what is going on. We notice what's happening in us and around us, whereas, at one time maybe we wouldn't have noticed. However, through gradually understanding ourselves in a new way, we come into a happiness and a profound way of being in the world that can't be so easily knocked off course.

Sometimes we may think we're not getting anything done in our practice, even though we're practicing quite seriously. In addition, maybe there are things happening in our life that are uncomfortable and distracting for us. We don't like them and we want to get rid of them. In resting, no matter what comes up, we get more and more of a sense that everything is equal and even. Open intelligence—or awareness or anything else it might be named—is indivisible, equal and even.

This beautiful practice gives us an opportunity to see just who we are and to understand the energies that appear in us and to make them workable. The practice leads us to find that all the energy in us is great bliss. If we don't yet feel that way, it's because of the way we have been trained, which is to think otherwise. But believe me, we can go far beyond our previous training in reification.

187

The way to do so is through vulnerability and allowing everything to be unpredictable. When we see that we don't need to manage what is going on, we understand correctly. I realized at some point in my early life that I was using countless maneuvers to try to handle things. I had thought that I needed to be working on things all the time in order to harmonize them, but I found that this isn't the case at all.

For certain, there have been miserable times in my life, very miserable times. There were times much earlier in my life when I felt like I wasn't going to make it. I simply had no idea how to live in the way I wanted to live. But most fortunately, through this process of letting everything be *as it is*, something incredible began to open up. Even though something might have seemed very scary, it could have a significantly different outcome than the one that was envisioned.

During one period when I was a young adult, I was so tortured and had no idea what to do in terms of living my life. My mother sent me a book called *Power in Praise*, which was a book about gratitude and praising God for things that we don't like. There was a specific prayer in which one would name the afflictive event and then give thanks to God: "I'm in misery. Thank you for this event."

Even though it was way outside my wheelhouse to take on something like this, I was willing to try anything. I even followed my mother's advice! Yes, I followed her advice, and she was right on target. This approach to prayer really altered my attitude, and shortly after taking this on, I had a tremendous opening.

Any kind of commitment to love is good; however, love that we didn't ask for or require is really the best. Through the practice we find a love we didn't know was possible. This is the love that belongs to open intelligence. It is an uncontrived, non-grasping love that is unbidden. It is something we did not make up with our mind, as in, "I will love this person if they love me."

Unbidden love is the love that is settled, quiet and selfless, the love that is the intrinsic energy of who we are. The more we are able to relate to the energies in us and to rest in those energies, the more we can experience this selfless love ourselves and then give it to others. If we are partnered or married, with unbidden love we have so much more to give there as well.

We have learned to identify certain feelings in our body with particular emotions. For example, there is an energy state of emotion that is called "falling in love." When we fall in love, this energy state becomes full blown; however, it is often only on the emotional level, and this very intense emotion of "falling in love" won't last. In order to find the real substance of the feeling of falling in love, we need to see it for what it is: an energy that is not defined by any label or circumstance.

It's so important for us to deeply understand that we are the site of incredible power. It isn't like some kind of cut-off spiritual power; it is the inherent power in us. We *are* creative energy; we are the inherent power to create. When we come to this rich insight, we learn more about how to express our own creative energy. We come to know ourselves as being free from our made-up ideas about reality. To be raw and real in this creative energy is humbling. It doesn't have a self-important way of being; instead, it is humbling.

The best way to normalize things is through letting everything be *as it is*, but in addition, we can get to know ourselves through normalizing what's going on with us in a group setting. The Twelve Empowerments (*the introductory teachings*) are such a process of normalization, because we have a skilled process where we can clearly see our own data. We look deeply into our own experience and write things out completely and thoroughly, and then we hear from others about their own experience.

This is such a rich forum in which to have things normalized, because we see that we are not the singular expression of exceptionality that we thought we were! We see that others are having the same experiences we are having and that we are not alone. This is another gift that the teachings are bringing to us: an ability to listen very keenly to ourselves and to others and to acknowledge the shared experience.

❧

In terms of my own exploratory process, I started relying on the unconscious when I was very young in the way of saying, "How can the unconscious help guide me in living my life?" In some ways I trusted the unconscious more than I trusted anything else. I knew that the unconscious would offer insights that were beyond my conceptual understanding. This is the importance of symbolic content, like with dreams.

Of course, all of our content is symbolic, but dreams come freely and unexpectedly and are not altered by us or anyone else. No matter what it is, it is symbolic of us. It's never symbolic of anyone else, even if we dream of other people.

I feel that there's a certain aspect of working with the unconscious that is very difficult to describe, because it isn't conceptual at all. It's more of a way of being without all the conceptual strategies and the make-believe reality that get in the way. The unconscious contains very personal content that is extremely evocative of emotion as well as things that seem chaotic and disorderly.

The unconscious grants us insight about how to deal with these things and to skillfully direct our life. I believe the guru often acts like the unconscious and may even be the voice of the unconscious for us when it comes to certain things. Gurus are meant to be entirely spontaneous, just like the unconscious.

Dreams are in this way important as guidance tools. If anyone wants to hear the inner voice, dreams are a great way to do it. They are a very effective way of dealing with the enthralling illusion that we have been involved with all of our lives. The more familiar we are with our dreams, the more we realize that they are our friends.

The more we give to a friendship, the more likely it is that the other person will want to be friendly with us as well. So also, with dreams. As a trusted friend, dreams can guide and instruct us. Dreams need to be handled within the unique context of the person experiencing the dream. Even if five people had exactly the same dream, the meaning would be unique to each individual.

❈

Dreams are symbolic in their expression, and all of my life I have thought about things through symbols. Early on this is how I created order for myself: by having my own set of symbols. They gave me a sense of autonomy and sovereignty, and this was extremely important for me, because I derived my meaning from these symbols. In symbols we find another way to think about things, a way that is representative of our genuine self. Because I have become so familiar with symbols and their meaning, I sometimes see things in a way that maybe others don't see. We are each unique, so of course we would also be unique in the menu of symbols we use.

We have had a global system of symbols and signs, many of them scientific or mathematical. Music and mathematics are fundamental languages of humankind, and people who work in mathematics and in the arts are working with the signs and symbols of those areas. One of the beautiful things about thinking in images and symbols is that it's much easier to see the pattern within everything that makes it all work together. This is what omniscience is: seeing and knowing the pattern in everything that makes it all work together.

All living systems have an orderedness that pervades everything. This all-pervasive orderedness cannot be done away with. In seeing these inherent patterns, there is a greater and greater resonance with who we truly are. In being resonant with this intelligence, we can give ourselves more fully to it, and most specifically in the things we most like to do. Some are artists, some musicians, some writers and some have multiple areas of knowledge they have a command in, but whatever the area of interest, with practice there is greater resonance with the core intelligence.

We have assumed that we think only in terms of words, but now there is more and more evidence which states that the way human beings really think is through symbols. Words are symbols too, of course, but words are abstract, so it's more difficult to attune them to the heart. Gurus speak using a lot of signs and symbols, but in order to understand the power that is in them, we must be able to see everything *as it is.*

When we think about some of these things from a scientific perspective, for example the one provided by quantum physics, we can see that things pervade each other and are totally interconnected. If the body is looked at under an electron microscope, the body is seen not as something solid, but as filled with space. So, space is the essence of the body when viewed from the vantage of an electron microscope. These insights are very convincing symbols for me in terms of identifying meaning, and this is what has been of interest to me all of my life.

When it comes right down to it, whatever else we may take away from the teachings, one key thing is insight. Maybe first there is intuition, then we begin to have insight. We are empowered with intuition, insight and interpretive ability. So, in acknowledgement of this great empowerment, we practice.

No one here can say, "I can't do the practice." I have complete faith in you. You can borrow my faith if you feel that you don't have enough faith yourself. It's all a single power, so it doesn't matter where we get it or where we think it's coming from.

A LIFE OF EXCITING MYSTERY

CHAPTER THIRTY-ONE

We don't need to be the creator of knowledge, because the required knowledge already exists. This lessens our burden to know. To realize that all knowledge already exists leads us into a life of exciting mystery!

When we are introduced to the teachings, we have chosen to be introduced. We are ourselves taking that action, and no one is doing anything to us. We choose to make ourselves available for the introduction, but we also have to be open and respectful enough to receive the introduction. It would not be possible to be fully introduced if resistance were predominant.

Due to a lifetime of reification, we may come to the introduction with a certain ignorance, or one could call it innocence, about our own true nature. Even if we had a bit of an idea about our true nature, it was likely not clear to us, and there was little support to bring us to a more clarified view. But with practice, realization is slowly revealed. It is fortunate that it is usually revealed gradually, because if it were revealed all at once, it would be challenging for most people, just because we have been habituated to a certain way of seeing things.

Through the introduction, we are being called to examine, investigate and realize the highest energy in everything that is perceived. Everything we see is our own space of exaltation, a space that is more comprehensive than the blur of colors relating only to the objects we perceive through our senses.

In the West especially, awareness is described as a cognitive process, with the cognitive gears creating self-awareness and awareness of objects. That's a totally dry definition and holds no appeal for me. I don't want more of merely cognitive ideas.

We can't bring about a rearrangement of all our points of view that is going to come together and constitute fundamental truth. Instead of expecting that, we enjoy the colorful display and know it for what it is and for what it is not. Every appearance in this vast display is pervaded by the utter lucidity of open intelligence. Here we rest completely, without any need to make the appearance into a multiplication of ideas.

When we realize everything to be *as it is*, we realize ourselves to be as we truly are. Really the only place of warmth and comfort in life is in our ability to connect with what's real and then speak from there and exhibit qualities from that space. We are not achieving some goal of betterment, because we're not a self-improvement project.

Regardless of what anyone else is doing or what society is telling us, when we rest as we are, the foundation of what we experience and the way we describe ourselves becomes exalted. As we rest with the power of who we've always been, we begin to acknowledge ourselves as the powerful creator of our own reality. We come to know ourselves as filled with qualities and activities that we could never have known through reification.

⊕∞⊕

It would be good to take our most troublesome energy, whatever we think causes us the greatest pain, and to practice with it. We can rest with even the most afflictive things that come up, such as, "I feel depressed, I feel hopeless, I feel rejected," or whatever it might be, and see it as an experience that has its origin in open intelligence.

The thought or emotion that has arisen will pass, and that can be counted on. If we investigate our thinking very closely, it's easy to see that it comes and goes and that each thought is energy. It has never become a thing; it has always been sublime energy.

For each person, there are exalted qualities and activities that are called forth by resting, but so often we don't believe we can have these qualities or activities. Because of the incessant troubling and self-critical voice in our heads it seems impossible that we could bring forth these qualities and activities. This is the voice that has been given to us through reification and binary thinking, but it doesn't mean that it is our true voice.

Most of us grow up in situations where we experience lots of criticism, both from outside and from within ourselves, and it is from this that an incessant critical voice emerges. Self-affection really begins with feeling the depths of the self-critical attitudes that have been modeled for us, starting when we were very young. Later in life when yet more internal and external criticism is introduced into our lives, a feeling of self-contempt can build even further. It keeps getting stronger and stronger, until we have an entrenched self-critical attitude.

This attitude might lead us to think, "I can't do the things that others can," or, "I must be a loser." We end up trying to prove that we are not a loser, and that effort can lead us down an endless trail of misery. "Loser" is a very strong word, and when we think we are a loser, we don't believe we're worthy of love, and we don't believe we're worthy of doing well in life. This can often be very self-entrenched, and it's very difficult to rid oneself of it through the causal processes that are offered today.

To feel that one is not worthy is really pride and arrogance. It might seem like it is an act of belittling oneself, but it's actually a form of false pride. One feels oneself to be the only one unsuited to be included in the all of all. It is a way of feeling special in one's unsuited-ness, which is just the flipside of feeling special in one's pride and arrogance. To be the only one excluded would be impossible. No one could possibly be left out, and the logic in this is so simple that it could be understood by anyone.

The practice of short moments offers complete love, without any way out. We couldn't get out if we tried. Why? Because this complete love is who we are. The love of the true self is not a love like any other love; it is the space we occupy. Love is everywhere and it's never separate or gone; it doesn't come or go or increase or decrease. It is completely spacious and completely deep.

When it comes to diligence and practice, it really doesn't need to look any particular way. We are each very nuanced and we each practice in a unique way, so to compare oneself to someone else isn't needed. When we first begin to practice, we have no idea what the fruition will be. However, people gradually recognize that through rest they're able to do things they once couldn't do.

When we gain full confidence in our practice, we find more and more that we're okay with everything that comes up. Practice is absolutely key to this feeling of okay-ness, of basic goodness, because for so long we have been trained to not feel good about ourselves. All of our most deeply held ideas about ourselves can now be left behind, and we don't need to depend on them anymore.

The realization of self-love through practice is the root of compassion. It isn't something we have to cook up. When we feel love, we act compassionately both towards ourselves and towards others, and this becomes more and more spontaneous and automatic. When we have a sincere wish for everyone to be happy and free, things look quite a bit different when compared to when we were walking around scowling at people.

We as individual human beings have a particular purpose, and we come to know what our purpose is from what we love. That's how we know what our purpose is—from what we dearly love.

We have to look at things from the perspective of what we love, and that is one of our entry points to the nature of mind.

As practitioners we know for sure that each instant is completely unique. There's no way to hold anything in place. The practice of letting it all be *as it is* allows our view to become more and more lucid. This is essential for human beings at this time. We are going through tremendous change as a human community, and we have no idea of what is to come. We see that *everyone* is in peril. This is the reality that we're facing, and it is very important to find a practice that soothes and guides.

In this time of great change, the things in life we have relied on before won't be reliable; they just won't be. We might as well start practicing now, if we haven't been. Or if we've practiced only a little, we ramp it up. It's fine to start small even with one moment, as long as it's built every day—quantity, quantity, quantity. Many short moments, repeated many times, are like drops becoming a great ocean. The key is quantity, not quality.

❁

Knowledge is already spontaneous in the universe; all knowledge whatsoever already is the universe. When humans discover what to them is "new" knowledge, it isn't new knowledge to the universe. The universe already holds the knowledge. In that sense, we can know anything we need to know about anything. We're always that broader perspective spanning multiple domains of intelligence, with human intelligence being only a small slice of the whole.

This idea that all knowledge already exists and that the entire universe is made of knowledge and that all of this knowledge is available to us means that we can receive anything. We don't need to be the creator of knowledge, because the required knowledge already exists. This lessens our burden to know. To realize that all knowledge already exists leads us into a life of exciting mystery.

Even though we think we might need to travel a distance to reach something, awareness never goes anywhere. By genuinely relaxing, we begin to withdraw from the idea that we are seeing something far away. The seer, the seeing and the seen are occurring within our awareness.

We are not concrete individual entities, nor are we merely discrete images. The more we rest, the more that we can see that all phenomena are emanations of all-encompassing light rather than discrete images. The tight grip we have had on ourselves as being a separate body and mind can relax. We are aware, without awareness any longer being distracted or misfocused.

That doesn't mean we never have a thought, and it doesn't mean that we never have any kind of afflictive energy coming up, because we will still experience those things, but our relationship to them is so very different.

What is seen is the joyful unfolding of the intelligence that is always present. Resting as this, we are able to enjoy the decisive realization that for everyone knowledge is spontaneous in the moment. It is not a privileged position for only a few.

The Ultimate Solution

CHAPTER THIRTY-TWO

What we need to do is practice, and whatever comes out of that practice will come. Resting naturally is the ultimate solution. If we are experiencing turmoil, the solution is to rest.

This is a time of great discord and dispute in the world, and one aspect of this is the online realm, which is filled with blame and hatred. People are expressing themselves without inhibition, and their expression is evidence of what the person is practicing according to their present circumstances and their particular pattern. They are practicing it for their own reasons. There's no way to eliminate the negative activity online; it's ramping up and it will continue to proliferate.

There may be people who have irked us on social media, and we may have never met them and don't know them at all. We don't like what they have said, or they said something about us that isn't true, but, well, there it is. Even though we may not agree with what they are doing and saying, they are another being just like us, and that is the basis of our relationship with them. That is to be honored.

It is not a matter of trying to figure out who they are or trying to make their opinions understandable to us or someone else. What we need to do is practice, and whatever comes out of that practice will come. Resting naturally is the ultimate solution. If we are experiencing turmoil, the solution is to rest.

We are not here to do things the "right" way or tell others what the "right" way is. We are not here to show how virtuous we are and how unvirtuous they are. We are not here to show that we have the best set of points of view. We simply are here as we are.

Human beings in general like kindness and harmony, and when there isn't kindness, it can really hurt. We're social beings, and we like to feel connected to others. Even if we are living alone in a cave, we are still a social being, because whoever we take ourselves to be in that cave has been socially constructed through the society we have lived in.

◈◈◈

We can never feel connected if we only remain rooted in the causal domain of "my opinion" and "your opinion." When we rest, we are everyone. This may just sound intellectual at first, but slowly through the practice we come to see that this is definitive. Through this we can know beings in a more profound way. If we look at things in a clear, comprehensive and kind way, we are prepared to receive what is coming our way.

What if we say to ourselves, "That annoying person can just be dismissed." Does that thought reflect the way things really are? No. No one can be dismissed from open intelligence. Even if there is the notion of dismissal or rejection, open intelligence is still present anyway. Through resting as the profound love within oneself, love is sustained, regardless of what is swirling about. This is a brilliant example of bodhicitta energy, the accommodation and potential for wisdom and skillful means.

Enmity, afflictions, happiness and all the rest are within us and aren't happening anywhere else. When we feel offended by someone, the offense isn't in them; it's in us. We're the ones who are feeling the offense. No matter what they do, they cannot *force* us to feel what we are feeling. We feel what we feel due to our own choices.

The ability to know exactly what is going on with us comes from deep self-inquiry, and not from intellectual speculation. Be gentle with whom you conceive yourself to be and whom you conceive the other to be, and in doing so this leads to natural gentleness and compassion for all. We're not self-centered in our realization. The enlightenment of all beings is what we are practicing, and this emphasis takes the focus away from the individual self and all of its many concerns.

I am not suggesting here that we try to paint everything with rosy colors and then see things only in that way. If there is a harmful threat present for us or someone else, then proper measures must be taken. No one should tolerate abuse or exploitation, and those who are in a vulnerable position must be protected. If a person has caused harm, that person needs to be held responsible and prevented from causing further harm.

Someone who has experienced harm from another person has no control over the response of the person who has harmed them. The perpetrator may deny they have done anything or even blame the victim. The harm has been done, but in this present moment, what is the most skillful choice in terms of dealing with the feelings that come up in the aftermath of a harmful event?

Of course, feelings such as, "I hate him. He'll never be anything else. We should lock him up and forget him," can naturally come up and are totally understandable. However, it is in a sincere tenderness of heart that the fear and pain that were induced by this horrible event will no longer have sway. A person who has experienced harm can frankly acknowledge the raging emotions and at the same time see that there is also another path that is available: "Right now, can I have genuine compassion for the person who perpetrated this?" Please know that I am speaking from my own direct experience here.

It is the tender heart that has the ability to heal. One feels the deep pain of existence through tenderness, rather than subjugating another individual to hatred and revenge. Some people can stir things up terribly and bring great harm to others, and certainly there are things that are absolutely unacceptable and inappropriate. We have to recognize those things for what they are, and this is where skillful means based on insight and compassion very much come into play.

It is so very supportive and helpful to be able to be free of ideas about being restricted by a particular time or space. No matter how awful a circumstance might have been for us, it is possible to practice. I really do feel we need to challenge the notion that harmful circumstances can master us and keep us from well-being.

To practice we need motivation, and "motivation" means that we practice short moments whether we want to or not. The more pain we experience, the more motivated we are to practice. When we don't give up, and we have the courage to stay put with the practice no matter what happens, we see the results.

When we practice in our daily situation, things begin to open up, and we see that all of what we are experiencing is the dynamic energy of our own awareness and is never anything else. The dynamic energy is the seat of sublime qualities and activities. As we rest, and rest, and rest some more, we find a new kind of energy that isn't really a "thing" and which can't be measured.

Each moment we practice, we are displaying qualities and activities, and then with more practice, the sublime qualities and activities are available ongoingly. We are who we are, and there is nothing to do and no one to do it, so, why not just relax into our basic state?

Through resting naturally, we find a self-affection based on the happiness in perfect love, rather than trying to find a situation that fits into our preconception of love. We are present in all circumstances as a force of the dynamic energy of omniscience. We don't need to make an effort for anything or try to drive our mind towards a consequence. All knowledge needed in the moment is available.

We begin to develop trust, until that trust is fully fruited. Actually, it is already fully fruited, but because our thinking has been operating based on causation, it seems like we're bringing it about somehow or that something is happening to bring it about. But the trust, confidence and perfect love are being evoked and not created anew.

❧

If we do not acknowledge the impermanence of things, we suffer. If we don't have a profound understanding of impermanence, the solution is to practice to the point of recognition. To really understand who we are and to also be who we are, we need to be able to rest as our own suffering and to not avoid it or compel it to be anything different. Indeed, we rest naturally as our own suffering, and in this way, we connect with all other beings who are suffering. Not only human beings, but all beings. The Earth herself is a being.

Suffering is an energy; it isn't anything we can ever grasp or hold on to, and just like anything else, it doesn't have an independent nature. But at the same time, in the course of our lives, it needs to be addressed. This practice isn't a spiritual bypass, and afflictive emotions should not be avoided. Everything that comes up is faced totally and not avoided. Potency of action, exaltation and skillful means are discovered in whatever is occurring in life.

The end of suffering is in the moment; it isn't an event in the future. If we really look at our experience, how could we ever find a future? The future is a fleeting concept, just like any other concept. We might have an expectation about the future, but we never know what will happen. The best way to be fully present is in a short moment, and then to understand that no moment needs to look any kind of way. It's not boxed into a specific unit of time or circumstance. The moment gives us an opportunity to simply be as we are.

All of this, no matter what it is—pain, suffering, worries, pleasure, love—is the expression of *what is* in every single instant. There is no more learning. What would there be to learn when everything instantaneously resolves into the clear light of open intelligence? There's nothing to resolve. What always is, is what is shining forth right now.

Section Five:

GOING TO ANY LENGTHS

33. Wisdom Agency	208
34. What We Were Born to Be	214
35. Omniscience	219
36. The Primordial Sound	224
37. The Breath Practice	231
38. The Twelve Empowerments	237
39. In My Essence I Am Free	245
40. Great Love and Great Bliss	250
41. This One Great Choice	256

WISDOM AGENCY

CHAPTER THIRTY-THREE

When we rest for a short moment, we are serving ourselves, but at the same time we're serving all beings. Why? Because we are non-separate from all beings. What fills all beings fills us too.

In contemporary society we have learned that we only get ahead through work, effort and competition, and we have been taught that exertion, determination and productivity lead to fulfillment and happiness. But now we're getting in touch with the fact that we already are complete and that we have nothing to effort for.

We have been searching for a reward, but at the same time we were afraid that we would be punished for failure. This kind of mindset diminishes us, and it keeps us bound in a very, very small domain of intelligence. We need to discover that we exist within countless domains of intelligence throughout innumerable infinities, and it is helpful for us to consider how vastly more encompassing our mind can be.

If we have a subtle bias or even contempt for what we don't already know, how can we possibly be open to the miraculous nature of all things? How could we possibly be open to the fact of our mind being present in all domains throughout innumerable infinities? Our mind exists everywhere, but in order to see this, we must remain open to the possibility.

Our limited causal perceptions are only an illusion. There is no way to substantiate and verify time and space or causality, because ultimately they are an illusion. They are illusions most fundamentally, just like a mirage. As unbelievable as this may sound, it can be realized in our own experience.

If we have an image in the mind, it is a mirage. What happens to it? It spontaneously resolves, just like a mirage disappearing from sight. We might think we have a mind full of all kinds of thoughts and that these thoughts that are appearing give meaning to life. False. That is not the reality.

When we investigate our mind, we see that a thought comes up and then it disappears, and there is no independent self-identity that made it happen. If we really want to know what our true identity is, why don't we begin with the idea of being a primordial agent of wisdom. We are always wisdom agents and we are never any other kind of agent.

❧

If we fill our minds with illusory things and we tell ourselves that somehow these things can harm us or fix us, well, that leads to the utter confusion that we see in the world. Instead of confusion, what we want to communicate to the world is wisdom agency. Wisdom agency is unbearably compassionate, and as wisdom agents, we allow that unbearable compassion to shine forth.

There is no longer a need to parse and nuance things with binary ideas. If we simply allow ourselves to rest, we are resting in a space of omniscience, and we can rest no matter where we are. The sign of accomplishment is omniscience, and it's clear when omniscience has taken place because of the results of its actions in the world. Whatever our passionate interest is, that's one place where omniscience can appear.

We have wanted to fit in with other people, and as a result, in order to feel safe in the human community, we stepped away from the omniscience we were born with. For a child, feeling safe is very important, and one of the ways a child tries to create safety is by replicating the behavior of adults. But now with the practice, we no longer seek safety in adherence to imposed norms and we return to our innate omniscience. The practice that brings us to this recognition is a very sublime gift.

The result of omniscience is knowing what to do and how to act. But please don't think that knowing what to do and how to act in every situation will mean that everyone in the world will suddenly say, "Oh look, wow, that person is omniscient." It doesn't mean that at all, because the concept of omniscience is something that is currently very unfamiliar to the world.

Omniscience can look all sorts of ways. It can look totally foolish and out of control, and yet still be completely omniscient. This defies all our rationalistic ideas. In fact, this is the disproving of and melting away of our rationalist ideas. Omniscience is always in the context of unbearable compassion. The face of omniscience is unbearable compassion. If someone wants to practice to the sign of accomplishment, the way to go about it is to practice unbearable compassion.

We all have access to omniscience. It's our birthright, and through practice we realize this directly. Wherever we go, whatever our career is, it will fill up with omniscience without even trying. We'll be able to see in our lives all kinds of things we could never see before.

The language of Dzogchen is changing in accordance with its presence now in the modern world, like language among humans has changed all along. Right now the language of the world is one way, but already it's changing. With the vantage that is demonstrated in this new language of open intelligence, one can see the demarcation between a unified way of looking at things, as opposed to rationalistic thought based on objective knowledge, cause and effect, time and space. Another aspect of this new vantage is a lessening need to "succeed" through competition and seduction. To compete and to seduce has been the subtle form of getting what we want.

The problems of the world—climate change, racial injustice, economic injustice, gender injustice—are products of rationalist thinking. We are facing huge issues and they are only just beginning. If we think the pandemic is horrible and we think the rising of the oceans is horrible, just wait! But you see, it is not all doom and gloom. Why would we want to continue in a way that has not provided solutions when we can clearly see a much better way that brings about benefit for humankind?

Knowing what to do and how to act has no plan. It is absolutely spontaneous and without conventional limitation. We greet everything spontaneously in the moment with full confidence that we know what to do and how to act, without ever thinking about it. It can be wild and brilliant and can appear in any way possible. Enlightened expression is not something that's controllable, whether it's in writing or speaking or in some other form. Whatever it is, it can't be made into a preconceived idea or plan, and this can be very startling at first.

❦

When we rest for a short moment, we are serving ourselves, but at the same time we're serving all beings. Why? Because we are non-separate from all beings. What fills all beings fills us too. These energies are shared energies.

It's not helpful to label people with totalizing concepts. We need to simply meet people where they are and value them and realize that they have the same potential that we have. They aren't different, they aren't other. All human beings are precious.

When we are coming from binary thinking and are engulfed by the competition, seduction and anger that go with it, that is a welcome occasion to examine whether this has worked for us. If we look in the mirror we'll see what we look like when we are spouting our negative ideas about ourselves and others.

When we fall into negativity, it shows in our face, it shows in our body, it shows in the way we look at other people and how we are with all people. But there is another way. When we are melted into the warmth of the heart, we look at everyone with unbearable compassion, and there isn't anyone or anything that can be left out.

Through the practice we find a richness that we had not known before. We no longer feel compelled to make ourselves into "someone." Rather than suffering all the disappointments that come from being someone, we have the experience of being awestruck at whatever we are beholding.

※

Aggression is the expression of anger and anguish, and the expression of anger and anguish can sometimes be extreme. This is why the Dalai Lama has said, "A single instant of aggression can ruin one's entire life." This is an absolute statement, and we can see how it might play out. Aggression is very, very precarious.

If we have an arising of anger and aggression and if we allow that seed to flourish, we have to recognize that it could cause great harm. It's very important to be aware of the initial aggressive act, which always arises first in thought, and only afterwards in action. If we are really angry and we build that energy into something, we need to be vigilant, because one seed of anger can ruin someone's life completely and everything they've worked to attain. This is true, and unfortunately I have seen it happen.

With the anger comes the tendency to think about ourselves as an individual agent acting in the world, when in fact our agency is the wisdom of omniscience, which is not merely a practical or conventional wisdom, but sublime wisdom.

In the practice we cut through all of the ideas we've accumulated along the way. If we know the teachings, we know their power, and we're fully vested with that power to practice. Keep it this simple, as simple as possible.

WHAT WE WERE BORN TO BE

CHAPTER THIRTY-FOUR

We open up to aspects of ourselves that we have been denying ourselves without even knowing that we have done so. We have no idea that we have incredible power within us—power to enact inconceivable activities.

For most of our lives, we have not known about the possibility of seeing things in a new way. Even though lucidity and clarity are native to us and we experienced them during the early years of our infancy, as a result of our early miseducation, we no longer know how to access them. But now the energies in our body need to be seen in a new way, free from imposed labeling. As we practice, we become more sensitive to our energies, and we can see what it is within us that we want to meet.

When energy comes up in us, like for example the impulse to anger, it is an energy that does not yet have a name, until it is named, as say, "anger." When anger and aggression come up, they must be skillfully dealt with. We need to rest in the energy itself, *as it is*, and not be carried away by a mislabeled notion that can harm us and harm others. The resolution of aggression and anger is the platform for realization.

We sometimes have flutters or even explosions of energies that we at one time in our lives might have felt frantic to get rid of or which we wanted to turn into something else. But because we are resting now, there's no longer a frenzy. We rest while we realize that "frenzy" is like the beautiful plumage of the peacock. An ancient legend states that the peacock drinks poison and from the poison itself comes the peacock's beautiful plumage.

Similarly, we rest as whatever afflictive emotion is appearing, and in doing so we can realize its actual nature. Then the energy becomes for us an adornment, like the peacock's plumage. This

214

is a surprisingly straightforward thing to do once we have been alerted to the possibility.

⊰◦⊱

It is important to know how to rest when the first twinge of an emotion comes up. It could be an emotion that is obvious to us right away, or it could be something we've never noticed, but either way, this energy has the potential to express itself at some point. Through skillfully encountering the feeling energies in the body, we initiate a process of practice that inspires us to experience ourselves and the world in a new way.

To be completely enthralled to the labeled emotions like arrogance, pride, envy, jealousy, anger, fear, hope and desire is a bit crazy. Why do we do it then? Because we have so very much engaged with them in the hope that the emotional states that we identify as positive will continue and that the negative ones will all go away. But that has never happened for anyone, so how could it happen for us?

When we practice, we bring the power of realization to the positive and the negative points of view, but also to the things we don't remember about ourselves from the time of infancy and to the pivotal notions that have formed our identity along the way. We might be somewhat aware of them, but maybe we've never experienced them at a feeling level in our body.

🛆

So then, there are basically two ways of experiencing life. One is a rationalist way with causally-driven ideas describing everything as binary—good and bad, want and don't want, reward and punishment, realization and no realization. This way of being is the result of the naming and labeling of things we received in our upbringing.

The second way of experiencing life is through a more comprehensive intelligence, an intelligence that allows us to be in a way that is not accessible through binary thinking. This doesn't mean that binary idea-making is completely left behind or eradicated. It means that binary thinking can be applied to certain patterns of knowledge, but it is no longer the only knowledge available.

When we are no longer looking at things through a binary lens such that we are trying to divide everything into good and bad and so forth, we really settle into ourselves. We realize we've never been this individualized self-identity trying to get something done and that we have just been trained to think that we are that way.

In the teachings, this is called "crossing over," which is transitioning from rationalism to a more comprehensive way of thinking about things. Then comes "direct crossing" or "direct transcendence," which is the practice of the direct perception of pristine consciousness. One aspect of this is that one begins to be *that which sees through colors*, rather than merely observing colors in forms. This is the recognition that the appearances that seem to be outside oneself are in fact the presence of an awareness that has no inside or outside.

The core elements of the teachings, such as cutting through and crossing over, need to be repeatedly heard again and again, over and over again. Repetition furthers; every time an aspect of the teachings is heard and then heard again, it furthers the accommodation of the teachings. The teachings and the practice aren't really taken in so much through thoughts, but rather through this increasing accommodation, which is a sort of increasing familiarity with the atmosphere of luminous mind itself.

Over and over again these same teachings are repeated. Rightly so. Repetition furthers. Repetition furthers. Repetition furthers.

❀

Emptiness, or better said, the accommodation and the potential of all data, is the very presence of the luminous mind. Emptiness—accommodation and potential—is not a place that is somewhere else. When our understanding of emptiness is not merely an intellectual concept, but one which fills our lived experience, this allows us to more skillfully deal with our thoughts and emotions. This could be a tough task for overly intellectualized Westerners; however, I don't think it needs to be a tough task any longer.

Whatever form these teachings may take, in the end they say essentially the same thing. Even if practitioners are practicing in different ways, they are sharing a common core experience. We want to be able to understand with authenticity who we are and who others are from this vantage of common experience. No matter who we are, we share the same mind. It isn't a different mind like "your mind" and "my mind." We have the same mind, and through devotion to the practice, we realize that this is what our common experience is.

As devotion to the practice takes root in us, we know for sure that truth is being revealed. We start to feel an energy that is unlike anything that we felt before. Many people feel much more exuberant and filled with vibrant energy. They have the ability to understand life and to live it in an extraordinarily vital way. That is my own experience and what I see in many others.

Do not expect to be ecstatic all the time, but do expect to be profound and sublime. "Ecstatic" is just an emotion. When we can relate to the energy of the emotion rather than the name of it, that is when we really begin to understand things in an entirely new way.

❀

We investigate our own minds and find that we can definitively see that each datum that appears spontaneously releases without anything needing to be done. Eventually, we realize that this is all that is occurring, and we can relax. We recognize that there's no way to control the spontaneous arising of thought, and what is more, that there is no need to control it.

Our idea that we have chains of thoughts that are informing us and that each chain of thought somehow relates to the others is an erroneous assumption. A thought comes about instantaneously, and we might recognize it and give it value—or not—and then it's gone, and the next thought comes. These are not connected to each other.

In fact, if you want to know the whole truth of the matter, not only has the thought process been misinterpreted, but also the assumption of what a human being is. The human being, along with all perceived things, is essentially like a dream. We are like a mirage: we seem to appear, and then that appearance spontaneously self-releases. However fantastical this statement may seem to be, it deserves to be investigated.

We're now putting words to the energy *as it is*, rather than as it isn't. We aren't choosing to practice binary thinking and emotionality any longer. Now we choose to be expressive through the heart, the center of all profundity and sublimity. We can be entirely devoted to our own realization and devoted in the same way to others.

OMNISCIENCE

CHAPTER THIRTY-FIVE

Omniscience is a depthful way of knowing with nothing in the way. It isn't a production of thoughts; it is the spontaneous presence in short moments. When we practice a short moment, we are practicing a short moment of omniscience.

One could say that a short moment is a reminder to ourselves of who we are, but yet, we aren't really *doing* anything in the short moment. We're showing up completely, that's all. It's really open intelligence that is doing all the work. When we practice short moments, we're learning to consider things in this new way.

As we practice, our own energy—the energy that is always already here, always free and complete and brimming over with omniscience all the while—becomes more and more obvious. Each short moment is an opportunity to reveal an entirely different way of being. It is a way we're born with, and it is the way we likely knew when we were very small children.

The ability to meet who we are in such a direct way and to see that the sign of accomplishment is possible for us could be seen as a goal of practice. However, to tell you the truth, I don't really practice with any goals. I practice guru devotion and I practice to die well. That's my short moment. I share the teachings through devotion to my gurus.

True knowledge is omniscience, and whether we believe it or not, each of us is in our essence omniscient. This needs to really be investigated, even if one was not educated to consider oneself to be omniscient. If you presently do not feel you are essentially omniscient, be prepared to be surprised!

In both the East and the West, many people are confused about omniscience. Why? Because almost everyone has been trained up in seeing themselves as a localized entity that is limited and not omniscient, and that they could never be any different. We've heard that only God is omniscient and that human beings can never be omniscient. So, we're definitely confronting and challenging a lot of cultural beliefs we have had.

❧

There is a "new" intelligence, at least new to us, that is much more comprehensive than the way we've learned to think. This "new" intelligence is what we're adopting in the teachings. In each short moment we're adopting omniscience. I feel that anyone who practices ongoingly will begin to see this sign of accomplishment. What is most important for us is to practice everywhere and in all circumstances and to never stop practicing, come what may.

Omniscience is a depthful way of knowing with nothing in the way. It isn't a production of thoughts; it is the spontaneous presence in short moments. When we practice a short moment, we are practicing a short moment of omniscience, and we become familiar with a space we probably did not know existed. We find energy within that is calm and powerful. Most of us have not learned that this is a possibility. When we do, we may jump for joy!

Omniscience allows us to solve the issues we couldn't solve with rationalist, binary thinking. It doesn't matter who we are; we could be a laborer, a businessperson, a doctor or anything else, and suddenly we could determine a whole new way of doing things. It could be something that had never been done before.

Omniscience is the sign of accomplishment in Dzogchen, and once omniscience is discovered, it's always-on, so we can apply it as we like. To be clear, we do not focus on "gaining" omniscience. Instead, we focus on the practice, and omniscience is simply revealed as a full-blown reality. It becomes very obvious and there's no question about it.

It is commonly thought that omniscience is a divine state where everything is known, and indeed, in my youth I had also looked at omniscience in this totalizing way. Instead, it is a matter of knowing what is needed in each moment. "Knowing what is needed in the moment" means knowing how to be and what to do right here and now, and the more proficient we are in practice, the more we know what to do in the moment.

Again, what is needed to be known is known *in the moment.* "Knowing in the moment" doesn't come from a train of thoughts that we add together, and it is not an accumulation of information. It also does not come about through studying something. It is simply knowing, ultimate knowing.

We have a deep sense of meaning occurring within us when we're in touch with the energy in our body. We have a felt sense of the primordial energy in our body and know that this is the location of what is called enlightenment or omniscience. Omniscience isn't an idealized place that is somewhere else.

In the first moment of introduction we begin to become familiar with this, and not after a lifetime of practice. We're introduced to it right up front. In each short moment we take, it is a short moment leading us to omniscience. Omniscience is already the case, but because we aren't yet convinced of that, we have to prove it to ourselves through practice.

People all over the world have suffered together in the pandemic, and we feel bonded in our common suffering. The human condition is one of suffering, and many people are suffering terribly. The more familiar we are with suffering, the more we have the invitation to practice compassion and kindness. It is from omniscience that the skillful means to relieve suffering will arise.

Avoiding suffering doesn't lead anywhere other than wanting to try to avoid more suffering. The teachings promise us an end to suffering. They don't state, "Just some people can end suffering and others can't." It's possible for everyone. Along with stating that suffering exists, it is pointed out that there is a path to enlightenment for us to tread and a release from suffering. Keep practicing in whichever way suits you best, that's the key.

I was born with some kind of inability to stay separate from the anguish that others feel and that I feel too. When I was younger, I would have a strong physical and energetic response to suffering, and I would receive all kinds of negative feedback about it, as in, "Stop being so reactive and emotional." But have any of us ever been able to stop the feelings that naturally arise? I wanted to really understand why I had such a strong response to suffering, and I wanted to have the knowledge and capacity— what I would later know to be omniscience—to serve suffering beings.

We have learned in the past to describe our energy in a way that it isn't, but now we can reclaim our energy. One of the ways we reclaim our energy is to realize unbearable compassion. Unbearable compassion is equal to omniscience; omniscience is equal to unbearable compassion. Unbearable compassion means having a beautiful connection with oneself and with others.

Unbearable compassion is the impulse, the commitment, the vow to protect all beings, and to make sure that all beings are afforded an opportunity to know themselves in this way. This knowledge of ourselves is the vehicle for our connection with others and our beneficial service to them.

As we go along in these years to come, unbearable compassion will become more and more important, just like it is in each of our lives as we participate in this practice. Unbearable compassion carries the energy of great love, great bliss and primordial wisdom.

Unbearable compassion is the birthplace of omniscience. Omniscience and unbearable compassion are synonymous. The living energy of omniscience is unbearable compassion. Omniscience gives us the ability to use our gifts fully and to use them in very unexpected ways.

In practicing unbearable compassion, we know where to go and how to act when we're there. This is also what omniscience is: knowing what to do and how to act in the moment in a way that's entirely beneficial.

THE PRIMORDIAL SOUND

CHAPTER THIRTY-SIX

When we meditate on sound, we're actually hearing the quiet of our own sound within us. We're listening to the sound of ourselves! Primordial sound is at the foundation of who we are. Primordial sound isn't the sound we ordinarily hear; it is the sound of sound.

Primordial sound includes all sounds, all descriptions, all manifestations—everything that we describe as anything. If we have a thought enter our minds, its description occurs as a sound. It has a name, and it cannot have that name without the sound that describes it.

As a reflection in water disappears of its own accord, false appearances fade away when their lack of reality is understood. How could they have any power? Their power comes only from creating a chain of thoughts to describe reality. At their basis is the primordial sound of open intelligence.

When we meditate on sound, we're actually hearing the quiet of the sound within us. We're listening to the sound of ourselves! Primordial sound—open intelligence—is the foundation of who we are. Primordial sound isn't the sound we ordinarily hear; *it is the sound of sound*. It is spontaneously present, it is free, and it never is anything other than itself.

Many times we have very strong reactions to the sounds we are hearing. Someone could say, "I love you," and we interpret the sound one way; someone else could say, "I hate you," and we would interpret sound another way, but the key thing here is that the primordial sound is present in both.

⊕∞⊕

When babies are born, they don't have any capacity yet to name things; for them there is only the unbridled energy of sound. They cry, then they're happy, and then they're in-between. Infants do not perceive a self at all. They see everything as an energy field, and they don't need to describe it at all. They don't think of themselves as being anything in particular. We love them and fawn over them because they are such great gurus in that way!

For them there is sound with no definition. They have no language to describe the appearances, but over time they come to identify themselves through what is spoken about them and to them. Even though babies are born free of any kind of bodily perception, they lose that because the urge develops to fit in and be accepted by those around them who believe in the existence of their own bodies.

We believe the sounds—the words—that are communicated to us. Everything we have thought to be true from a reified perspective came from this mindset into which we were trained. In a sense we copy those around us with whom we want to fit in; we duplicate what they're doing in order to belong.

We are taught that things have a form and that we have feelings and sensations, and through these we learn to interpret the world. We see separated beings and events, and the more we see separated beings and events, the more uncomfortable we feel, because intuitively we know that we are something greater than the individualized being we have been taught that we are.

We were trained to interpret sounds—and also colors—in a certain way, and through this our self-identity took shape, along with the way that we would represent and interpret the world. We heard more words that further elaborated our self-identity, and we were shaped to be someone.

It's very, very rare for anyone to have a clear understanding of what was taking place, but over time and through continued practice, we gradually begin to relate more with the primordial sound rather than with the causal sound. We're not trying to get rid of causal sound; we're resting as acausal sound—a sound without a cause.

When we apply oppositional thinking to everything, we don't feel comfortable at all. There's a din in our ears brought about by this oppositional thinking, and maybe we've never noticed this din because it has been so obvious. We have had the sounds pressing on us due to habit. That's what it is: habit. The teachings have to do with the exhaustion of oppositional thinking, the exhaustion of data and the release from repetitive habits. What this really means is the exhaustion of the din of reification and oppositional thinking.

We begin to notice the din that is associated with the rush to causality and oppositional thinking, and we allow the din to resolve. If there is a disturbing thought that comes up, the practice is to see the "disturbance" as being the same as any other sound. Relax and let the sound resolve into the primordial open-intelligence sound that is infinite.

When we rest profoundly, we realize that the din disappears into primordial sound. This is all happening within us; we're not going anywhere, like to the heaven of primordial sound. We are already in the heaven of primordial sound. This must be realized in experience, as there is no way to understand this from a merely intellectual perspective.

Let's say that we have an impulse. Right away what happens is that we speed towards that impulse and then towards causal interpretation. We feel the speed of energy going towards an expression of sound that is associated with causality. However, when we rest, instead of going off with the speediness, we rest as the primordial sound that is the basis for the description.

We hear the din and then rest with it. We find a completely different way of interpreting sound. We notice the energy in our body and get to know how it runs throughout our body. We can take any troublesome idea and practice with it. Everything becomes still, and soon we are able to rest with the speedy energy that comes up, and we begin to feel the self-affection that comes through the practice of sound. We had previously been cut off from self-affection because we have never actually heard who we truly are.

But now we want to describe ourselves from the space of what we really are, not the space of "You're something small and damaged and apart from anything that is sublime." In the self-affection that comes from this discovery we fully enter sublimity, because we're no longer applying notions we have acquired that diminish us. We know how we have felt when we attached oppositional thinking to everything—binary ideas of good and bad, reward and punishment, right and wrong and so forth—and we don't want that for ourselves any longer.

With soft breathing, we are resting with the speed that is trying to take over. With the soft breathing in and out, we feel the energy running through all of our body. When we use this breathing practice over and over again, we can recognize the speedy energy that comes from the reification of sound. When we rest as the energy of the speediness, it resolves into its primordial essence of sound—open intelligence—rather than having the mind run wild based on what it is thinking.

When we rest as sound, we become aware of the sound many of us have never heard before. As the relative sound dissipates and becomes less obvious, we are recognizing primordial sound, and that's what we get in touch with. Because we investigate and examine it in our own experience, we can see the distinction between primordial sound and relative sound.

Rather than practicing with sound as being outside the body, it is good to practice sound with the energy of the body. We usually relate to the sound we hear from outside, but we are ourselves always sounding. The energy of that sound in our bodies isn't just in our ear, it is everywhere. At the same time, we need to be sure that we are rooted in our body and that we are practicing in a deeply somatic kind of way, because we also live in these bodies moment-to-moment.

When we rest, we feel a release from our worries about the reified sounds we have identified with. We feel something happening that we didn't recognize before, which is the union of great bliss and emptiness. The experience of great bliss is a feeling of warmth that sweeps over everything, a warmth that fills space.

As we rest, everything settles down, because we no longer rush into the speed of these things that have been so very bothersome. Instead, we experience them resolving in a very direct way. With this we are invited to enter into the meditative state of primordial sound.

❁

Whatever is heard, it is in its essence the sound of sound. It is the sound of the empty place, the unknowable place, the ineffable place, the open-intelligence place. The primordial sound of emptiness has no material substance. Even though everything is subsumed within it, the sublime emptiness never becomes anything else. It simply pervades everything without ever becoming it.

When we practice sound, we see ourselves as the sound, rather than as something merely embodied. This is how we realize in ourselves the power that is at the source—the primordial sound. We are it. We are the rhythm of the sound. At first it may look like we're hearing something external; however, prior to the subject who is hearing and the object that is heard is the primordial sound itself.

We are resting as the great emptiness, also called the accommodation and potential of all. We come to see that sound is the expression of emptiness. We may think that we're observing something, but with the simplicity of the practice, we soon realize that there isn't an observer or experiencer; rather, the sound is who we are.

By resting as sound, we come to realize that no matter what it is we're saying or doing, it carries the heart essence. Primordial sound is never separated from great bliss, from the heart essence of what is called "emptiness." We can call it "the heart essence of primordial sound." It is the accommodation and potential for everything we know and everything we've ever thought about or done.

Over time, the way we look at things changes, and then suddenly, *boom*, the recognition comes about, just like that. The practice of sound opens up enlightened speech, and there's only open-ended knowledge creation after that. Through the resolution of the sounds that we had used before to describe our experience, we express ourselves in a different way. It can happen instantaneously for some, and then for most others it is more gradual.

ཨོཾ

OM is the seed syllable and comes at the beginning of most mantras. OM is the accommodation and potential for all else to appear—the visual and audible representation of primordial sound. OM is really inexpressible, but it represents the realization of emptiness. OM is very, very significant. OM is the sound of warmth and devotion, the sound of love. It is deep and vast and contains all sound and subsumes it.

A mantra is the most powerful means of soothing the mind. When we practice with a mantra, sometimes it's tempting to think about it as applying to the mind alone. However, when you practice with a mantra, feel how the mantra soothes body, speech and mind. Reciting a mantra evokes an energy that is of inconceivable power.

THE BREATH PRACTICE

CHAPTER THIRTY-SEVEN

The breath becomes our identity, and in that recognition it's much easier to really understand what it means to be the primordial space of everything. We're not cut off in a human body, as if the universe were unfolding on its own as something apart from us.

It is important to be introduced to the practice of breath. When we breathe, we feel the rhythm of life—the breath going in and out, in and out, in and out, until the last breath. We breathe, we rest, and we come to see the attention to the breath as a way of resting. How very essential it is for us to nurture ourselves in this way of resting through the breath.

We are using the breath here in such a purposeful way. We are becoming familiar with the breath being the life force of everything, and not just our own life force. This is a practice that is very much based on the energy in the body and how the energy in a human is united with all energy.

We want to respect our place in the natural world and unite with everything in it. We want to have the same fondness and love for it as we do for ourselves, and not only that, for all beings seen and unseen, recognized and unrecognized.

Most of us have never learned how to truly calm ourselves, but here we are learning how to breathe so that there is serenity. The body has energy that is so entirely spacious and depthful, such that it could never be comprehended with thought. Simply by learning to breathe with full awareness, the entire body is filled with serene but extremely potent energy. These are energy practices not just in the body, but in the energy of everything. When we are practicing with our own energy, we definitively realize the energy of everything as singular and united with us.

In the breath practice we don't have a lot of thinking. We're breathing with full awareness, but without thought or hope or desire. In doing the practice, the somatic aspect calms down, and we can feel that taking place within us. We feel a sense of gentleness and peace, but we might also feel fire and power too. The practice of breathing out into the open space of great completion allows us to be with things as they actually are.

❧

The first thing we want to do in the practice is to simply place our attention on the breath, and as we breathe, we let our attention go out with the breath and dissolve into the space around us. The breath enters, but it isn't an abrupt or heedless in-breath. It's a gentle entry of the breath into the lungs and then down to an inch or two below the navel. The breathing is with the entire torso rather than only in a shallow way.

Usually when we breathe, we breathe in, and as soon as we have finished breathing in, we immediately start breathing out. Then as soon as we have finished breathing out, we start breathing in again. There is not any space between the in-breath and the out-breath. However, in this practice, we breathe in, hold the breath a bit, and when it feels comfortable, we breathe out gently. Then we breathe in again gently, hold the breath for a bit, and breath out slowly. As we breathe in and out, we rest the mind in open space.

This aspect of the teachings is called "mixing mind and space." The "space" is the space of indestructibility, of indivisibility, of ineffability and of spontaneity. We don't have to try to make any of these things occur, because they are already present.

The breath is soft and it is taken in attentively, and not in the manner of frantic breathing, as is so often the case. With practice this gentle and attentive way of breathing becomes the natural way that you breathe. Breathe in once again, and then as you breathe out, place your attention again on the outbreath, following it out and mixing mind with space. Rest in that open awareness.

If you do this in a gentle way, you will feel the energy come up and fill your mind and body. You'll feel it, and it is soft, gentle and warm. The breath is like a steed, and the mind rides on the back of the breath-steed.

Breathe in and then breathe out into vast space. In doing so, let everything be *as it is* and feel the energy going up and down. When we do the breath practice, the energy opens up. There isn't a need to engage in any kind of conceptual process. The vast space into which we are breathing becomes our identity, and then it's much easier to really understand what it means to be the primordial space of everything.

⚇

It is a form of meditation to see the mind as the breath, so when we breathe in and out, our experience is that awareness is all-pervasive of our breath, and our breath is an aspect of all-pervasive awareness. It is a way of meditating that is very profound.

With the practice of breathing out into the open space of great completion, it allows us to be with things as they actually are. As we continue with the breath practice, more and more we begin to see things we did not see before. What is more, we don't need to be afraid to acknowledge what is going on with us, even if we have extreme afflictive states that are arising.

With breath practice, we get to the point where thinking begins to slow down. It doesn't mean that there aren't any thoughts; it means that we're not commenting on the thoughts with more thoughts. We resolve the mistake of labeling our emotions with descriptions that cause us pain and harm.

When we practice, we do not have to contrive positive feelings about anything, and we don't have to combat negative ones either. We don't need to make the negative ones different, and we don't need to make the positive ones a source of desire. The more we practice with the breath, the more we feel competent to deal with anything. And when we feel like we are struggling in our practice, what do we do? We keep practicing.

❀

We come to realize that we are exalted and that we have within us the power for sublime activities unlike anything we have ever carried out. As we go deeper into the breath practice, we find wisdom-exaltation, which is an expression of realization.

The breath becomes our identity, and in that recognition it's much easier to really understand what it means to be the primordial space of everything. We're not cut off in a human body, as if the universe were unfolding on its own as something apart from us. It is very important to understand that the primordial space is not merely an object of our attention, but is our own open-intelligence selves.

We're relating to the heart-space, breathing with the heart, and speaking to people from our heart instead of our head—connecting with other people and feeling close and safe. We're exalting ourselves by seeing that our profoundly beautiful, sublime energy is in whatever is occurring, because the primordial space of everything has brought forth the energy of what is occurring. There aren't any enemies. The only "enemy" we have is our own misunderstanding.

❀

This is not a mindfulness practice. Mindfulness is an effort, and what we are speaking about here is spontaneous and effortless. So, there's nothing to do. We usually think that there is something to do and something to be gained simply because we were educated in a binary way of thinking. We lost track along the way; we lost the golden gossamer thread somehow, but now through practice we've picked the thread up again.

The "picking up of the thread" means that it is important to include every aspect of life in our practice—walking around, doing the dishes, doing laundry, washing the car, etc. Each person has subtleties and nuances in their life and tasks that aren't the same as anyone else, so these are honored, and at the same time we remember what the basic practice is.

We're skillfully supporting ourselves by seeing that our profoundly beautiful and sublime energy is in whatever is occurring. The accomplishment is in feeling the release from thinking, thinking, thinking about everything. It is the release from any kind of notion that realization is to be found in the mental life of reified thinking. Realization pervades the mental life, but the mental life can't build anything that it isn't. So, we can find some relief in that fact.

I feel that the breath practice is the practice for these modern times. It is a practice that everyone on earth can do. The approach of mixing the mind with the breath is one of the main meditation practices taught now in the West. When we do this practice, we know we're joining other practitioners and also people all over the world, because people in Eastern cultures have been practicing this meditation for many hundreds of years.

One need not practice with ambition or with a goal or the feeling, "I am going to achieve something with this." I would say that my goal, if it could be called a "goal" at all, is to die well. That's what the Tibetan gurus have all practiced—to die well. In Tibetan culture there are many practitioners who practice to die well. In death so many things come up that we would never expect. How could we know for sure what they will be; we haven't been dead yet!

There will be surprising things, and there will be all kinds of phantasmagoric images stirred up in us at that time. Instead of shrinking the quality of our life as we move into death, we exalt the quality of our life into death. We practice in life, and then we can practice into death.

THE TWELVE EMPOWERMENTS

CHAPTER THIRTY-EIGHT

Whether we allow open intelligence to be obvious as our lifestyle and encourage it or we do not, at the moment of death, what is completely obvious is open intelligence, and nothing else. At that moment we will remember those Empowerments.

The Twelve Empowerments are a twelve-part training that introduces a participant to these teachings. The Empowerments are an introduction to the practice of natural rest and how we can rest naturally in all daily activities. They show us how living a life based on data has affected our own lives and our relationships with others, and how we can now become complete in those relationships.

The purpose of the Twelve Empowerments is empowerment! The beauty of the Empowerments is that they lead us to a life where we're no longer being blindsided by our data. We get to see that what we have called past, present and future has always been pure wisdom magic.

The Empowerments are a process that opens up the capacity to rest profoundly—even for people who are absolutely certain that it's totally impossible for them to rest. In the Empowerments we gain direct insight into the nature of experience. We can see whether our vantage is coming from reified data streams or from realization. In realization we have no position on anything; we're entirely impartial.

I would like to talk a little bit about how the Empowerments are related to these teachings and how they are practiced. I would like to go through the first few Empowerments and share their essence. Even though the Empowerments are stated in a specific and concise way, the richness and depth of each one is revealed throughout all of life. Each one is so profound.

When the Empowerments were first written, I had spent more than a year traveling, and I had set out on this trip thinking, "I have found satisfaction and flourishing in my life. There must be many other people who have found the same thing, and I am going to go out and meet them." My trip didn't turn out as I had planned, but in the course of things I saw that what the world needed most of all was a simple training in the nature of mind.

By the end of the trip I felt that the best thing to do would be to start a series of teachings. They were first called "The Twelve Inquires," but were later renamed "The Twelve Empowerments." We scheduled the first one, and I had no idea what to write for it. The night before the First Inquiry, I sat at my desk and started writing until I stopped writing. I wrote the text and then I wrote the questions at the end.

The next day we offered that First Inquiry in a group, and I sat and listened to everyone share the answers to the questions. From everyone's responses and sharing, I knew what was needed for the Second Inquiry, and from there on out, I prepared each subsequent Inquiry from what became evident from the previous ones.

⊛⋙⊛

In the very briefest form, this is what the Twelve Empowerments point to:

1. Empowerment One: What includes all data?

2. Empowerment Two: What is the natural state?

3. Empowerment Three: How do data shine forth in open intelligence?

4. Empowerment Four: What about us does not emphasize reified data?

5. Empowerment Five: What about us is all-inclusive?

6. Empowerment Six: What is unstopped?

7. Empowerment Seven: What is absolutely reliable?

8. Empowerment Eight: What about us is naturally beneficial?

9. Empowerment Nine: What has no other?

10. Empowerment Ten: What is perfectly clear?

11. Empowerment Eleven: What is spontaneously present?

12. Empowerment Twelve: What is indestructible?

The Twelve Empowerments are the starting point for the ultimate care of the self. They are a life review, but they are unlike any other life review we have ever participated in, because they show us that we are perfect as we are. All the other crazy ideas we have and all the baggage we've been carrying around about who we are and who we aren't are ideas that are based on reification. These reified ideas do not have truth value.

The Empowerments require openness, and that means entering into the introduction to open intelligence with no preconceived notions. Usually when we begin to learn about something, we have to accumulate certain knowledge before we can go on. So, the prerequisite in that case would be an accumulation of knowledge, but the only prerequisite for the best possible experience with the Empowerments is simply, again, openness with no preconceived notions. Anyone can muster that up.

Everyone has the same potential to be introduced to open intelligence, but not everyone has the same openness. With a little encouragement openness can come about. What is required is for the teacher to first create a communication bridge, which requires knowing what the participants are interested in and where they're coming from. Then, by standing in their own place with them, we can go forward from where they are into complete openness with no preconceived notions.

The Empowerments aren't a one-time play date. They can be returned to again and again. If there is something difficult in life going on that you can't quite figure out or some kind of conduct that you don't really want to be engaging in—but you're engaging in it anyway—then revisiting the Empowerments will be incredibly beneficial, because the issue can be cleared up. We won't have to be vague about things any longer.

The First Empowerment begins with a very profound question: "What includes all data?" In Empowerment One we take responsibility for all our data streams. What does that mean? It means no one else caused them and will not cause them in the future. No one can cure them, and no one can control them. When we reach this point of understanding, we realize that all these disparate ideas about who we are couldn't possibly be who we are.

There is an introduction to open intelligence in the initial training before we start the Empowerments, so we have been introduced to the idea that open intelligence includes all data. The way that I approach this inquiry is to think, "All data are included in open intelligence, and so I need to practice as the energy of the data and not on the basis of the names and descriptions of the data." We have had a great propensity in our lives to either get away from or run towards things. Instead, now we rest without drifting to one pole or the other, and we're seeing that we are not just helpless victims of our experience.

It would be good to give an example of how Empowerment One can play out in a specific life circumstance. I was once in a business arrangement with a man who had definitely hurt other people in a significant way through fraud; however, I had no feeling of anger towards the man. I felt love for everyone in the situation, including him.

When we're able to see exactly what's going on, then solutions come that are out of the ordinary. In an arbitration that came about due to the actions of this man, I said, "Everyone here is responsible in some way for what happened, so we each need to pay the investors based on our involvement." So, that is what happened, and there were folks who had to pay significant amounts of money.

I was the only one there who said something like this, and I had no idea whatsoever going into the arbitration that I would say these things. None. As it turned out, my statement was very well received, and in implementing it things worked out okay. As soon as I said what I said, which took about one minute, I could see that the people involved were relieved of any kind of fear about what to do.

It wasn't like this man was easy to get along with. There were all kinds of things going on all the time. It was up to me to practice with my own data. In a very practical way I was supported by my practice, and never was there an instant of going into any kind of resentment, fear, chaos or disordered thinking about the situation and this man.

In the arbitration, I took responsibility for everything that was going on for me: how the investors felt, how all my friends involved in this felt, then their families, their finances, how they're going to be affected by what's happening, and so on. If any of us were to be in a group like this in the future, it would be ideal to have one person who could connect with the situation in a thoroughgoing way, such that a solution could be readily found. To be fully present with everything is the essence of Empowerment One. We take responsibility for our data streams, no matter what they are.

☙

In Empowerment Two, we have the question: "What is the natural state?" In practicing this Empowerment, we start to believe that we actually have the power within us to be whole, to be centered and to take care of ourselves. When we rely on that power, the power increases. Short moments repeated many times—a cup is filled one drop at a time.

With Empowerment Two, it is a matter of deciding that things could be different through no longer avoiding or getting rid of things. Instead, we invite everything, knowing it will be the perfect practice of the moment. The question of this Empowerment, "What is the natural state?" prompts reflection. Its basic action results in a person beginning to feel promise. That's what I would say: beginning to feel promise through this knowledge and insight. Based on making the commitment to go forward in this way, there begins to be signs of accomplishment.

The Third Empowerment is: "How do data shine forth in open Intelligence?" We make a list of the behaviors that have separated us out from others. That's how we're going to see how our data have been shining forth up to that moment and how a new possibility has entered in. Let's take this example again from the arbitration: in that space with all those people who were involved, I needed to see that all the data that were arising were shining forth as open intelligence.

❁

The centering question in Empowerment Four is: "What about us does not emphasize reified data?" Empowerment Four is not about thinking about things ad nauseum and regretting how things have been. Instead, we make a very detailed list of how our way of engaging with data has played out for us and others. It is a matter of gaining insight. We do that by fully investigating our relationships and writing down everything that is going on— what we've been up to in our life, whom we've hurt, who has hurt us, and how exactly we have responded.

Empowerment Four can bring up a lot for participants. When I first looked into this, I found that I was really oblivious in some ways, so I sat down and I focused on how my actions had affected others, and through affecting them in whatever way that was, how I was affected too. I understood that I really needed to get clear about what I want to practice and not to drift into things that are merely conventional or popular.

Empowerment Five is, "What about us is all-inclusive?" If our actions have been coming from anger, irritation or annoyance, through this Empowerment we can really start to see these things clearly, because we now have a simple and clear way of looking at our lives. This is very important, because in the process of this Empowerment we tell other people things we have never told anyone. When we do so, we enter into inclusivity and commonality. Inclusion is not some kind of intellectual position; it is a skilled action.

In Empowerment Five we sit down with others and share everything about ourselves: good, bad, and indifferent, what we're really embarrassed about and think we'll never tell anyone, or whatever else it may be. We tell it all. Even if we don't tell it all at that point, we do get to a point where we can do so. We can admit things to ourselves and then be able to share these things with others. We might do this with some reluctance for some things, but so what? In the end it is the discovery and the honesty that are important.

ༀ

The more severe the afflictive state, the more incredible the wisdom, so there's nothing to hide out from. This is where Empowerments Four and Five are absolutely essential. By being completely open and honest in Empowerments One, Two and Three, we're able to list everything in Empowerment Four, if we dare, and that isn't only a one-time opportunity, but an opportunity that is always available.

When we look into our lives in the Empowerments, we are seeing that everything about our lives in the past, everything in the present and everything that will occur in the future has this ground of natural equalness and evenness. We give up our right to be a victim of anything that has occurred in the past, and that brave decision goes against the entire way we are trained to think about our identity as being the sum of everything that has occurred in the past.

In the Empowerments we realize the obviousness of open intelligence in every single aspect of our life. No matter how much enthusiasm or dread we have in regard to the Empowerments, and whether we think they're boring and meaningless or totally great, when it really gets down to it, the Empowerments are truly life-changing. Whether we allow open intelligence to be obvious as our lifestyle and encourage it or we do not, at the moment of death, what is completely obvious is open intelligence, and nothing else. At that moment we will remember the introduction to open intelligence that we had in those Empowerments.

IN MY ESSENCE I AM FREE

CHAPTER THIRTY-NINE

In a world filled with suffering, one may hear in some spiritual circles affirmations such as, "May I be free of this." That is all well and good, but why ask for something we already have? Since we are already free, why not acknowledge it in that way rather than pray for it like it's somewhere else?

We have been trained to be quite disturbed when afflictive states occur. Whether we realize it or not, when we are quite disturbed, we are continuously interpreting everything through hope, fear and aggression. We hope that something will happen, we fear that it won't, and then we might use aggression to protect ourselves because of our insecurity about what will happen or not happen. This guarantees that the disturbance will disturb us.

I can speak to my own experience here. With all of the things in my earlier life that I had used to represent myself—like being in the right clubs, being a certain sort of person and having the right possessions and circumstances—well, nothing worked. I felt such intense pain and suffering from those causal ideas that I didn't have a choice but to step away from engaging with them.

I was in so much pain that I really had to do something. I knew that this old life hadn't worked, and I had some idea of what would work, but I really didn't know how to cross over the bridge I needed to cross. I had to find my way into true well-being, and most fortunately that is what has happened for me, step-by-step.

All along we are always only the presentation of indivisible, perfect love. As we recognize our own profoundly gifted, loving nature, this enhances our state of being and the way we look at life. We can directly address the energy that we've always felt could disturb us. We have a fundamental flow of well-being, and when thoughts and moods come, we can welcome them rather than trying to push them away.

There isn't one way to be with everyone and everything. Whomever we're with and whatever situation we're facing, that particular circumstance requires a unique and spontaneous response specific to that situation. We carry our realization into the situation and then we respond to whatever is at hand. It isn't a matter of making a list beforehand with, "Oh, I'm going to do this, then I'll do that, and this will work it all out." There isn't any way to determine for certain what will be required.

❧

When we have a thought like, "I'm angry," what are we to do then? Do we launch into all kinds of activities that can hurt ourselves and others? No. Instead, we rely on what we know to be true. We're going to rely on the teachings, and this is how we become open and willing to trust what is being offered and to know ourselves in a new way. We're no longer knocked off balance by the descriptions of thoughts and emotions.

In the course of a human life, there are circumstances where we might feel very aggressive. We could choose to do mean things to those whom we see to be the originators of our pain, or we can make another choice. Where is the aggression actually? Once again, it's in us. It's not in the person provoking us; they didn't put their aggression into us. We have a choice about the aggressive energy we feel, and we know that it will not work to try to make the other person wrong and thereby justify our aggression. Instead, we rest while everything unfolds.

For many people who are aggressive, their aggressiveness comes from profound discontentment in life, and they have no idea what to do with the discontentment. Well, I am not in a position to judge, as I can relate to that state of being in my own life, and I'm sure many others can as well.

Why do people experience discontentment rather than happiness? Simply because they do not know they are already filled with happiness and joy at the deepest level of their being. We've all been in that place of unhappiness to one degree or another, but through practice we no longer need to reside there. We can see why the introduction to the practice would be such a relief.

In a fraction of a second we can have a change of attitude, and something very powerful can happen. We don't even really need to know what it is or figure it out exactly. We can just enjoy the mystery. As we become more familiar with a happiness that cannot be produced, our emotions, our sensations and our thinking begin to increasingly feel aligned with that natural happiness.

As our practice progresses, we become entirely vulnerable to what suffering is and how much suffering has affected our lives and the lives of others. We are now making a choice to not have our living energy distorted through the wish to avoid suffering. We are resting naturally, a rest which doesn't require any effort at all.

As we rest profoundly, we become more and more okay with a feeling of deep vulnerability. An aspect of accomplishment is being spontaneously vulnerable to any appearance whatsoever. It is known that whatever the appearance is, it can be seen as the energy of open intelligence.

By getting in touch with our own suffering, we can recognize the suffering of all human beings. Our own suffering needs to be equated with that of others. We come to deeply recognize that all beings suffer and that we are not the only ones.

We have all had radical disappointments throughout life. There are many disappointments all along the way from the time we were tiny. From the beginning of life we were born into pain and suffering. Just think; the first thing we did was scream, right? Along the way we develop hope that we will be happy and fear that we won't be. If a moment of happiness comes, we might try to hold on to it. "Oh I am going to hang on to this so that it stays with me." But it never does stay ongoingly, because everything is impermanent. The sadness is impermanent and the happiness is impermanent.

We can develop a deep sense of our own place in reality that doesn't see us as divided out from all other beings. We all feel energy within ourselves, but with practice it is seen to be united with everything and everyone. How could the energy be unique to us? We're all in this together. If we think we're the one who is separated out, well okay, that's one way of thinking about it that we have learned along the way.

By staying with the path and practicing as is suggested, what is called "omniscience" comes about. Omniscience points to the capacity to find solutions for situations, no matter what kind of situation—long and drawn out or short term. Most are short term and we do not have to face a long period of chaos and pain. But there are other times where a situation is long term, like having to live in a wartorn country, where there are missiles exploding and one never knows what's going to happen next, and there is a level of anxiety in the whole country.

We are faced with many problems right now, including global issues that cannot be resolved with causality-based intelligence. Solutions can come from a space of connection where we're committed to a common wish to alleviate suffering, or to say it another way, to alleviate the injustices that are the causes of people warring on each other.

It is also the fact that we go through ordeals, and as surprising as it may be to hear, these ordeals can end up being very transformational for us. I feel that the pandemic and the current world situation have the potential to be very transformational, because in this time of upheaval, people are beginning to seek a way out of suffering.

In terms of our own practice, we don't need to create anxiety for ourselves about what is coming. When we practice, we have a clear vision and power about how to proceed in these dire situations. It doesn't mean that the dire situations go away, but we know what is needed in the situation and what isn't. Our practice is to rest naturally in the moment and to respond skillfully.

❀

When we elevate ourselves out of the entanglement of suffering and we bring all the suffering with us—knowing it to be the heart essence—the suffering looks very different. To realize the heart essence of suffering we need to enter into suffering, and not only what it means to us, but what it means to everyone.

There is no ideology or theory that will resolve suffering, because ideologies are themselves expressions of suffering. When we resolve our own suffering, we are actually engaging in the resolving of the suffering of all, because there is only "the all."

In a world filled with suffering, one may hear affirmations in some spiritual circles such as, "May I be free of this." That is all well and good, but why ask for something we already have? Since we are already free, why not acknowledge it in that way, rather than praying for it as if it were somewhere else? So, rather than feeling, "There is something missing or wrong with me and that needs to be taken away," we can affirm, "In my essence I am free."

GREAT LOVE AND GREAT BLISS

CHAPTER FORTY

Everything is turned upside down and inside out, and at the same time, we live in great bliss and with a great responsiveness that is not cooked up. Who we truly are is being expressed throughout our entire day, even though it has nothing to do with days.

To meditate on great love and great bliss is a very potent type of meditation, and this doesn't require any special setting. It can occur whether sitting formally for meditation or in the short moments that we experience as we move through the day.

What's most important is to be introduced to our spontaneous presence as the complete bliss body. The gradual discovery of great love and great bliss is the most elevated practice there is. It could be called the ultimate practice.

Great love and great bliss is who we are. It's not somewhere else where we have to travel to, or something that we hope will come to us. It is already with us, within us. It is us! But we may be oblivious to the fact that great love and great bliss is ours all the while. It isn't ours just once in a while in a short moment, but all the while. A short moment is the brief instant of showing us that we already are who we are, and what we truly are can't be taken away from us.

Another term for great love and great bliss is ultimate compassion. Compassion is . . . well, that's in fact a complete sentence: "Compassion *is*!" Of course, it's great to practice practical compassion in hopes of benefiting others, but ultimately "compassion *is*." That is to say that it exists as itself and does not need to be created or contrived. At some point it is completely spontaneous and no longer needs to be practiced.

There's no one being compassionate and no one receiving compassion; compassion simply is. To be so embraced by compassion that there isn't anything else that exceeds it is what omniscience really means. It is the quality of the all-giving, all-accomplishing, all-creating motherly buddha that we are.

Ah yes, mothers. I think probably most mothers think about the future their children will have and the community of human beings their child will live in, and this concern is such great evidence of natural and spontaneous compassion. To whatever degree they can, mothers want to ensure that their children's future will be a good one.

❁∞❁

The pandemic brought about much greater awareness of what our actual situation in the world is and how the future will likely look. With ever-occurring pandemics, climate change and the many injustices like racial inequity, gender inequity and economic inequity, it might seem like disaster is in full expression. It doesn't seem like things could be worse, but of course, they could become worse.

We're facing a time of incredible crisis for human beings, and the only way to interrupt this cycle of human-created crises is to discover a way of being that is not dependent on the thinking that created the crises and that sustains the many injustices.

The thinking that created the problems is not the thinking that will solve them. We are now facing a threat to the survival of the human species, and never has the demand been greater for all human beings to respond skillfully and compassionately.

There are all kinds of descriptions of the mind, speech, body, qualities and activities that we have had throughout our lives, and now we have these new teachings which at first may seem quite unfamiliar and difficult to realize. This new way of thinking and being may seem almost like a betrayal of everything we had learned before about ourselves.

Yet, from the time we are first familiarized with the practice of short moments, we have the introduction to who we truly are. Our ordinary way of being—where we're trying to do everything all of the time in a certain ordered way—is gradually cast aside, and spontaneously we respond, with no plan.

The teachings point us to the realization that time and dimensionality do not exist in the way that we have taken them to be. In fact, there is not a single thing that has ever had an independent, self-generating existence. Without reliance on the usual parameters of time and space, how would we define ourselves and understand who we are?

🔔

Omniscience and buddhahood are equal. There is one word that describes buddhahood—omniscience. But omniscience doesn't mean "all-knowing," like we're taught when we're involved in theistic practices, where only God is all-knowing. Omniscience is the capacity to not restrict one's thinking or behavior with dualistic ideas. It is a knowing that has nothing in the way and that isn't a production of thoughts.

This doesn't mean that the recognition and expression will be the same for everyone. Each of us has our own flavor of this universal principle. We have the ability to live life spontaneously and freely as our genuine self, and we are not bound by the limitations of binary thinking. We are now being affirmed for who we are and no longer for who we are not.

We already are omniscient. It isn't a goal, and it isn't evading us and we're not trying to evade it. It is our nature, so we couldn't possibly evade it. When omniscience is realized, its demonstration is obvious to us. We recognize that we're omniscient because it is demonstrated, but that doesn't mean that one will necessarily appear omniscient to others.

Most of us have heard that omniscience is far away and unattainable. We never think of omniscience as the natural state of our being and that we each are inherently omniscient. Instead, we have characterized it as something special and apart from us.

When we rest naturally, we rest as omniscience. When omniscience manifests, it manifests spontaneously. Through practice we're getting accustomed to the flow of spontaneity. We're simply showing up spontaneously with the presence of sublime activities and exalted wisdom. Anything that is a tool for forwarding that is very important.

We start to know things that were impossible for us to know through causality and rationality, because the things we are coming to know are not based on causation and reason. For example, if we have a plan for a project that we're doing, we might think that it's going to take a lot of time to realize the plan, but then, *boom*, all of a sudden everything needed for the project is seen clearly in a flash. All aspects of it can be understood and carried out, and it may occur in a way that has never been conceived before.

That example is evidence of the demonstration I am speaking about. After a validation such as that in one's life, one can no longer doubt one's own capacity. I feel that as people realize their own omniscience, that realization encourages others to understand who they truly are and to ponder what their capacity might be. I believe that it is possible that the younger generation today may have a greater facility for this because of the times in which they live and what is now required of them.

The Dzogchen teachings always match the beings they're teaching. When we have an opportunity to receive teachings such as these, we are very, very fortunate. I feel extremely blessed to have been given this gift. The teachings are beautiful and give us hope, but the question naturally comes, "What use is this going to be in my everyday life?" That's the question most people ask, and rightly so.

The answer to that question comes from a persistent and unwavering practice that brings confidence and assurance with it. A tremendous energy of an intelligence that is beyond comprehension comes about, an intelligence that guarantees us an everyday life that is open and deep and that can serve us completely as well as serving everyone around us.

There is a confidence that develops, a confidence that could not be expected or predicted at all. So, whatever is going on in everyday life, whatever one is doing and no matter how disordered it might look and how it seems it couldn't possibly be working to achieve anything, there is nevertheless the trust that there is enlightened activity at the basis.

Eventually the practice becomes one of non-meditation. Non-meditation is a matter of being choicelessly and spontaneously present to all that is occurring. One's conduct is spontaneously expressive of beneficial intent. Whatever happens, happens, and there is the skill to respond to it. Even though non-meditation may initially seem impossible and even disconcerting, it is the essential way of being.

Everything is turned upside down and inside out, and at the same time, we live in great bliss and with a great responsiveness that is not cooked up. Who we truly are is being expressed throughout our entire day, even though it has nothing to do with days.

There is no way to fully control anything. When we reach the point of seeing that nothing can be fully controlled, we are just relaxing with whatever thought or emotion we are having and leaving it *as it is* without any practice. This is what is called "non-meditation." Getting to the point of non-meditation means that we no longer have to be "meditating" in the conventional use of the word to be meditating. It is the union of opposites—meditation and non-meditation.

THIS ONE GREAT CHOICE

CHAPTER FORTY-ONE

I'm willing to be with your suffering, not just mine, because I know through wisdom-insight that your suffering is mine. This unites me with you, and you with me, and with the suffering of everyone.

We need to ask ourselves how we want to live in this world. Every single instant we have a choice about what we will do. I took some time in my life to inquire into this, and I realized that my intention was most specifically two things: to bring about a more comprehensive mind that can respond to things as they are, and to end suffering for as many beings as I could. I'm still committed to both of those.

With the short moments practice, we've been given a great freedom to have a choice, and we are able to decide in each moment how we will be and what we will do. No one else can tell us how to live; we live our own life. My own experience is that the more that I practice, the more I have the sense that I'm responsible for my own life. We are all responsible for our own lives, and we would be well served to make use of the resources that are available to us in having an incredible life.

A short moment is a golden kernel of truth. Every single second we are deciding who we are and who we are meant to be, and as practitioners we're being called to be aware of this choice we have. It takes a warrior, because you see, life is rigorous and sometimes very demanding, and we want to be able to fully and courageously show up, whatever the circumstances may be.

You could say that in each moment we teach ourselves who we are. No one can ever determine for us who we are, not ever, no matter how powerful the force. We are complete, so there's never anything to fight against or strive for. Our toolbox is our enlightened mind, speech, body, qualities and activities, and the teachings give us direct access to that toolbox.

All the good qualities and activities that are talked about in the teachings rest in the understanding that, no matter what it is that is conceived or done, it is always the accommodation, potential and presence of open intelligence in our lives. This intelligence that inhabits everything is our own, but unfortunately it is not an intelligence that most people have been familiar with in their lives.

Our feeling energies are where we rest. There isn't some other place out there apart from us to rest in. If we are trying to imagine the vastness of things, we rest, and all will be revealed about what that vastness is. For each of us it has a unique meaning. We go out into the world with our unique energies and express them in our particular way.

⊛∞⊛

Regardless of what happens in our lives and in the world at large, we need to practice. This is absolutely key, because practice frees us from mere emotionalism. Our life up until we began practice had likely been ruled by thought and emotion, whether we knew it or not. However, when we rest moment-to-moment, we settle into the characteristics, qualities and activities that go far beyond emotionalism and conventional reason.

When we practice, we gradually give up the old mind and the old ideas. It might seem completely impossible to go from a mind based in conventional reason to one that is not bounded by reason. However, with practice, one moment at a time, we come to see that it is possible. We may need some support to open up our thinking more, because often we don't understand our potential to do so.

The true definition of moral agency is to have understanding and purpose based on wisdom and benefit for all. The idea that there is some kind of totalizing moral authority imposed on us from outside need no longer rule us. When we rest in ourselves, we become very clear on what our morals are; otherwise, they may be vague, and this vagueness is a result of the way we have been trained. If for some reason we are unclear as to what our present morals really are, they are revealed in each moment through our actions and expression.

I have all kinds of provocations every day and so does everyone else, but the important thing is what we do with those provocations. With continuing practice, we get to see how often we project our own stuff onto other people. A provocation may come forth, and through our miseducation in reification we feel like we have to name it. But do we have to name it anything? Shouldn't we instead breeze along through life recognizing the energy *as it is* and realizing who we truly are?

More and more people want to find another way of thinking about things, because gradually they are beginning to see that they need to do so in order to be at peace within themselves and to have peace in the world. Even if we are very active with all kinds of things in our busy lives, we need to take some time to really settle in and take a close look at things. We need to know that we're okay and that we're safe.

Sometimes things come up that are so extreme that it seems that there is no possible solution; however, even if something seems difficult and un-solvable, it can be addressed in practice. If something seems un-solvable, that means, "I do not know what to do with it yet, and I need help and support." Something may seem overwhelming, but that does not mean that it is.

When we have been practicing for a while, we may reach a time when things seem to be going a hundred miles an hour. It could seem like it is all out of control—coming, going, passing away, and then that over and over again, sometimes reaching a fever pitch. This too may feel overwhelming, but the more that we are able to let things be out of control from the stance of rest, the less we actually feel out of control. What a great expression of vulnerability and courage!

Instead, the energy in the body is allowed to flow along with everything else in the cosmos. We no longer can posit that there is an "other" or that we are "ourself." This is the point where omniscience starts to come about, and whatever area that we have our greatest strengths, in that area our genuine self becomes more apparent.

Once I was in a situation where I was with someone else who was completely out of control. My initial response to being with someone emotionally disturbed and who also had a violent edge was fear. What to do in a situation like this? Normally, what anyone would want to do is to get away. So, what did I do? The opposite. I was present to it.

What I found was that it didn't kill me. I have the moxie—we all do—to be completely present to the pain of others and to our own. The pain is a misnamed energy, that's all. The energy in the body is omniscient. It is great love and great bliss, and the access to this is in the pain, and not in avoiding the pain. This has to be experienced and cannot be merely theoretical. The suffering and the pain are in fact a gift, if we can see them for what they are.

❀

We have had the good fortune to be students of these very great beings who came from Tibet, and I love to listen to the stories of the old-time practitioners. To have these great beings in my life is really unspeakably profound and beautiful. It is the greatest sign of blessing and an extraordinary gift. What a tremendous teaching it is to know about their lives. There is an assurance along the way that many others will also come to receive the teachings on the nature of mind that we have received.

The Dalai Lama once said, "Compassion is a feeling from deep in the heart that you cannot bear others' sufferings without acting to relieve it." In realizing the depth of the suffering of human life in others, we become courageous enough to deal with our own suffering, face it straight on, and then get busy with the suffering of others. And so, for me, when I say "I love you," it means I connect with you on the very deepest level.

If we are facing something difficult and we feel that we cannot practice as we go through the tribulation, we can come to the point of challenging ourselves to reach out for support, when we've never done anything like that before. Up until now, we may have hidden our pain, or we thought that our pain was unique to us and that no one else would understand it or want to hear about it. But down deep we all so very much want connection with one another, and we find that connection in a place we never thought we'd find it—in being in the unbearable suffering of everyone.

I'm willing to be with your suffering, not just mine, because I know through wisdom-insight that your suffering is mine. This unites me with you, and you with me, and with the suffering of everyone. There is a call to love, which means that we enter into the suffering of all.

FURTHER RESOURCES

For those who would like to become more familiar with the Short Moments teachings, there is the shortmoments.com website, where a number of resources have been made available.

One can download the app and have instant access to community postings and updates about teachings on one's phone.

There is access to the Short Moments books, which can be downloaded free of charge.

A number of talks from Z. Rinpoche are available, again, for free.

For a person new to the teachings, there are links for online meetups on zoom, introductory trainings, local open meetings, clarity calls and the Twelve Empowerments training, as well as a link to schedule a free one-on-one call with a Short Moments trainer.

One will also find the schedule for trainings at the Short Moments Center in Sweden.

www.ingramcontent.com/pod-product-compliance
Lightning Source LLC
Chambersburg PA
CBHW072341090426
42741CB00012B/2871